HE CAME TO YOU SO THAT YOU MIGHT COME TO HIM

The Life and Teaching
of
St. Anthony of Padua

by
Lothar Hardick, O.F.M.

translation
by
Zachary Hayes, O.F.M.

Franciscan Herald Press
1434 West 51st Street
Chicago, Illinois 60609

Library of Congress Cataloging-in-Publication Data

Hardick, Lothar.
    [Er kam zu dir, damit du zu Ihm kämest. English]
    He came to you so that you might come to him: the life and
teaching of St. Anthony of Padua / by Lothar Hardick: translation
by Zachary Hayes.
        p. cm.
    Translation of: Er kam zu dir, damit du zu Ihm kämest.
    ISBN 0-8199-0954-8
    1. Anthony, of Padua, Saint. 1195-1231. I. Title.
BX4700.A6H3713   1989
282'.092—dc20
[B]

                                                    89-36226
                                                    CIP

MADE IN THE UNITED STATES OF AMERICA

FOREWORD

Popular opinion polls are very common today. If such a poll were to be conducted among Christians, what sort of response would we get to the following question: What do we know about Anthony of Padua? It would be easy to predict the result. Among those who have at least some knowledge about Anthony, certainly a very high percentage would answer that Anthony is the Saint who finds lost objects. A much smaller percentage would know something about his life. We might suppose that among these people, the so-called miracle of the ass would be the best known, followed by the sermon to the fish or the appearance of the child Jesus. But all of this is legendary material to a greater or lesser degree. Certainly we would find a very small number who would know that, despite all the legends, Anthony is, in fact, a Doctor of the Church. But who knows anything about the doctrine which Anthony had attempted to comunicate as a Doctor of the Church?

Is it true that the Saint who is known and appreciated as a universal helper in the every-day, trifling affairs of life is, for the most part, unknown in terms of his thought and doctrine, and in terms of the understanding of the faith which he attempted to communicate to others?

Any author should offer some explanation of his primary concerns in writing a book about an important personage. We will do this briefly here. The accounts of the life of St. Anthony are, for the most part, legendary in character. I have attempted to take even these legends seriously. But the leading question in my approach is not whether the events narrated actually happened as described. Rather, the question that stood in the foreground was: What can this particular account tell us about the person and the meaning of the Saint. This is a question about the deeper meaning of a legendary account. And when it seemed appropriate, I have used statements of the Saint himself to illustrate the particular situations of his life.

Anthony is known as a Doctor of the Church under the title "Teacher of the Gospel." In order to show, by at least a few examples, that he has much of value to offer us today, I have attempted to provide something of a thermatic presentation of the Saint's teaching in the second part of the book in order to communicate some sense of his teaching. Here I was able to rely on authentic documents such as those found in the sermon-outlines of the Saint. The vernacular version of the words of the Saint is based consistently on the translation from the sermon-outlines prepared by Father Sophronius Clasen, O.F.M. in: *Lehrer des Evangeliums*, Ausgewalte Texte aus den Predigten des hl. Antonious von Padua (Werl, 1954).

We hope that this book might restore something of the genuine, spiritual shape and meaning of the "Finder of Lost Things." We have chosen a statement of Anthony as the title of this book: "He came to you so that you might come to Him." That statement can be taken as the key to the dogmatic and ascetic teaching of the Saint.

Karlsruhe, October 4, 1985

Lothar Hardick, OFM

CONTENTS

Foreward iii

Part 1. The Life of St. Anthony 1

Ch. 1: Origin and attempts to find his
          own way 4

Ch. 2: Fernando becomes a Franciscan 17

Ch. 3: Apostolic work in upper Italy 32

Ch. 4: Anthony in Southern France 58

Ch. 5: Anthony becomes Provincial
          of the Romagna 73

Ch. 6: The last period of his life in Padua 90

Ch. 7: Return home to the Lord 106

Ch. 8: The Saint lives on 119

Part 2. Teacher of the Gospel 131

Ch. 1: The Sermons 133

Ch. 2: St. Anthony's theological style 137

Ch. 3: "The Son is the face of the Father" 140

Ch. 4: "If anyone wishes to pray or
          meditate better" 150

Ch. 5: "The exalted dignity of the sinner
          who repents" 163

Ch. 6: "The members of our body are,
          as it were, the garments of the soul" 173

CONTENTS

Part 1

The Life of

St. Anthony

In the case of most saints, the quality of the devotion directed to them expresses the essential characteristics of their spirituality, their work, and their basic intention. The patronal significance and the iconography associated with the saint plays a significant role. If we think of cases such as Vincent DePaul, Elisabeth of Thuringia, and Francis of Assisi, the type of devotion associated with each of them reveals clearly the main lines of the life and intent of the particular saint.

In the case of Anthony of Padua, there are no uniform lines in the patronal significance assigned to him or in the iconography that depicts him. At the present time, he is commonly thought of as the saint who finds lost objects. At an earlier time, he was considered more as the patron of lovers and of marriage, as a helper at time of birth, or as a help against infertility. This is certainly singular for a saint who, as a religious, desired to live without marriage for the sake of the Kingdom of God, and who, therefore, had no personal experience of such matters. Aside from this, he was called on against fever, against diabolic powers, and plagues among cattle. In this instance, the so-called "Blessing of Anthony" played an important role. He was also revered as the patron saint of people who live in mountainous areas.

This is but a small selection of the matters associated with Anthony. By the simple believers, he was seen above all as a sort of heavenly factotum who is useful in every sort of need and difficulty. And it must be said that there is no real basis in his life for the idea that he is the finder of lost objects even though that is the most important role attributed to him today. The way in which the Saint lives on in popular piety does not always correspond well with his earthly life.

If the patronal significance of St. Anthony is diverse, the qualities attributed to him in iconography are just as widespread. The earliest among the symbols used in reference to him is the book, which may be seen to represent his teaching, or more likely, to represent the book of Sacred Scripture. Since about 1400, the heart, the flame, and the lily occur. Sometimes one or the other of these is used alone; at other times, several of them are used simultaneously. Since the sixteenth-century, the cross is used, and finally the Child Jesus. The image of the Christ Child is often combined with one or more of the older symbols. Less frequently, and as a local usage, he is depicted as an admiral in a sea-battle against the Moslems.

It must be pointed out that the Child Jesus, which is the most common element in the iconography depicting Anthony at the present time, does not have an absolutely certain basis in the life of Anthony; for example, in some apparition of the Child Jesus. Besides, this particular symbol has been attributed to series of saints before finally being attached to Anthony. The popular legend followed this and filled out the empty space. The legend depicts an apparition of the Christ Child. Thus, with the passage of time, new elements were drawn into the life of Anthony, both with respect to the Child Jesus and with respect to Anthony's status as the finder of lost things.

It is noteworthy, however, that precisely the very late symbol which is based on a legend — that of the Christ Child — corresponds to one of the essential elements in the spirituality of Anthony, namely, his strong orientation to Christ, the incarnate Son of God. "He came to you, so that you might come to Him." This saying of the Saint can well serve as a key to many areas of the living spirituality represented in Anthony.

I.
ORIGIN AND ATTEMPTS TO FIND HIS OWN WAY

The Role of Legend

The love and veneration which past generations had for the saints makes it difficult for us today to arrive at the sort of exact, historical image of the saints that we would prefer. Usually we have information about the death and the final period of the life of a saint which is somewhat dependable. At this time people would have already become aware of some greatness in this person and would have taken more conscious care to record sayings and events. As one looked back at the life of the saint after his or her death, it would have become clear that there were many gaps in the information about the saint's life. Here the creative nature of legend would have proved to be helpful. The enthusiastic narrative of legend is not intended to falsify, but to enhance and to underscore those qualities which, from its viewpoint, seem to be most important.

Since the narrators were aware of many wonderful occurrences in the case of other saints, they borrowed many particular elements from those sources in order to enhance the image of this particular saint more richly. It was a time when no one desired to depict the saints in fixed, unchanging portraits. The saints were painted against a golden background. Thus, even the legends have their golden background. Writers of earlier ages were concerned with the "typical saint" as understood at that particular time. From that perspective, the individual character of a saint could fade into the background. Today we approach the lives of the mediaeval saints in particular from a more critical viewpoint. Our question is: "What really happened? Precisely when and how did it happen?" We seek the historical-critical truth. And when events cannot stand in the light of historical-critical questions, we conclude that the account does not contain the truth. Legend, however, is not so much concerned with depicting what actually happened in this particular life. It is more concerned with presenting the meaning of the life. And is not the meaning of a life the deeper truth? With this in mind, we ought, perhaps, to learn anew to read and to understand the ancient legends in order to come to terms with the deeper truth they contain.

Origin

In earlier times, when the use of family names was not yet customary, people were commonly named after the place in which they were born. This is true of the saints as well. Clearly there were exceptions to this. And Anthony was one of the exceptions. Anthony of Padua, as he is known for the most part, was not born in Padua. He spent only a very short period of his life in Padua, namely, the very end of it. He was born in Lisbon. For this reason, Portuguese biographies call him "Anthony of Lisbon."

In 1147, Lisbon was taken from the Mohammedans by the Christians. The city had been strongly influenced by the presence of the Crusaders. Traveling from France and Germany, they came to the aid of King Alphonse I (1139-1185) in his fight against the followers of Mohammed. Actually they had taken up the cross to win the holy places in Palestine for the Christian world. But they remained in Portugal and thus spared themselves the dangerous voyage to the Holy Land. King Alphonse had made them generous offers to stay in his land and help him. And they could soothe their consciences with the fact that they had fought the Mohammedans on the Iberian peninsula, and thus had been able to do something for the Christian faith.

Among the Crusaders who remained in Portugal, Martin, the father of St. Anthony must be included. As knight of King Alphonse, he was quite well-to-do. His wife, Maria, came from an aristocratic family.

Thus, Anthony was born into a wealthy and privileged family. In this sense, he fufilled an expectation strongly associated with holy persons in the Middle Ages: a saint "must" be at least of distinguished origin and ideally of aristocratic origin. This corresponded to the thought-patterns of the time which reflected the feudal structures. It was only after 1200 that people of common origin made their way into the calendar of saints with greater frequency.

But in the case of Anthony this origin was not enough for the legend. In its enthusiasm for the Saint, legend gave him an even more noble origin. Thus, it was claimed that his mother had a royal background. And with a bold unconcern for history, legend claimed further that Anthony's father was Count Godfrey of Bouillon (d.1100), who had led the first Crusade to Palestine when it was under the domination of the Mohammedans.

It is possible that this legendary material claimed that Anthony himself desired to go to the Mohammedan city of Morocco, not as a Crusader but as a missionary. It is typical of the formation of legend that events of its hero's later life should be seen in certain anticipatory signs from the time of his birth onward.

The year of Anthony's birth is uncertain. The most likely time would be the years between 1188 and 1195. The first "Book of Wonders" (*Liber miraculorum*), which comes from the years between 1367 and 1374, claims that Anthony died at the age of thirty-six. Since the date of his death is set with certainty on June 13, 1231, this would place his birth in the year 1195. Biographers of the twentieth-century (Vergilio Gamboso 1973 and Samuele Doimi 1975) believe that they have good grounds for placing the birth of Anthony in the year 1190. The critical edition of his sermons which appeared in 1979 accepts the year 1188 as possible.

Is the claim that Anthony was born on August 15, the feast of the Assumption of Mary into heaven, to be explained as an expression of the clear Marian orientation associated with Anthony? It certainly serves the purpose of legend to place the life of the holy hero under the sign of the unusual and supernatural from the very beginning. This happens in the claim that the bells of the cathedral of Lisbon announced his birth. The house in which the Saint was born stood to the west of the cathedral, very near to the main portal. Shortly after his birth, the child was baptized in the cathedral, which was named Se Patriarcal. He was named Fernando or Ferdinand, a name which means "bold fighter for peace." He lived up to this name, even in the time when he was called Anthony.

There were likely other children in Fernando's family. We have certain information about only one sister who was named Mary, and who died as a canoness in the cloister of St. Miguel in Lisbon in 1235. She was still living, therefore, when her brother was canonized on May 30, 1232.

We know hardly anything certain about the youth of St. Anthony. Here again legend intervenes and fills the gap with wonderful, inspirational stories appropriate to a life that was holy and unusual from the very beginning.

Fernando as a Field-Guard

It is said that one summer day, the father, Don Martino, took his son, Fernando, to his estate near Lisbon. The wheat field was ripe for the harvest, but large swarms of sparrows descended on the spikes of wheat to eat the grains. The father went out to find the attendant of the field to scare away the birds. Fernando was told to take on this job until the other man could be found. Fernando, therefore, ran through the field to scare the sparrows. But he soon became weary of this when he came across a chapel which he wished to visit. Was it curiosity, or did he wish to pray? He found a way to keep the sparrows away from the wheat field and still allow himself to enter the chapel. He summoned the sparrows to follow him, then he went into the chapel with the entire flock of birds. When all the birds were inside, he closed the doors and windows.

When his father returned, he was both amazed and embarrassed. His son was nowhere to be seen. But the sparrows were gone. He soon found the chapel. When he opened the door, it all became clear to him. The birds flew out into the open. There was his son.

The story has the ingredients of a fairy-tale: the obedient son who is torn between duty and desire; the clever young boy who knows how to take care of himself. With a sort of self-evident confidence, he does things that are possible only with the aid of supernatural gifts. Being holy since childhood, he is drawn to heavenly things, and heaven itself stands by him with miracles. It is a story that could well be told to children.The great wonder-worker who is invoked for even the most common-place concerns "must" have done marvelous things from the very beginning of his life.

Parental Home and School

Written around 1316, the strongly legendary biography "Benignitas" claims that Fernando manifested a noble disposition very early in life, and above all, that he helped the poor with gifts. Other biographies speak of the loving devotion to the Mother of God which was a living reality in his parental home. It is said that Fernando's mother was very pious. But it is not possible to say anything concrete about the influence of his parents on Fernando's religious development. With regard to this, we can do no more than guess.

But an uncle who was a canon did have a strong influence on Fernando. This is true not only with respect to the religous life, but with respect to studies as well. This fact would make its influence felt later in the life of the Saint. The uncle was a teacher at the cathedral school of Lisbon. When Fernando had reached the appropriate age, his parents sent him to this school, wherein the instruction included everything that was customary at such schools at that time. This would have been first the so-called trivium: grammar, dialectic, and rhetoric; and then the so-called quadrivium: arithmetic, astronomy, geometry, and music. All in all, it was a good and comprehensive education and training for the mind. Naturally, at a cathedral school, religion also would have been studied both as an academic discipline and as a practical matter in the celebration of the liturgical offices. The entire program was set up in such a way as to foster a decision to enter the religious state. Those who had an inclination toward ordination to the priesthood would be led in that direction through the study of theology. This was the case with Fernando.

Personal Temptation

The "Legenda Assidua" was written in 1232 and re-worked extensively in the course of the thirteenth century. In its account of the youth of Fernando this Legenda presents him as a young man who had to contend with very personal temptations. There we read the following: "When the temptations of the flesh were awakened in him with the onset of puberty and he felt tempted beyond his strength, still he did not fail in curbing his youthful desires. Each day the world offered him opportunities for the strangest experiences. Yet that foot which he had not yet placed firmly on the threshold he pulled back out of fear that some of the dirt of earthly pleasures would remain clinging to him and prove an obstacle for him who had already entered the way of the Lord with all his heart."

In an age familiar with the views of Sigmund Freud's theory of sexuality, many would like to have more detailed information about what is merely intimated here or described in very general terms. In his biography of the Saint written in 1570, Lorenzo Surio goes into greater detail. According to him, the matter deals with a young servant-girl in the house of Fernando's parents. She had fallen in love with this young man, who seemed so full of promise. Perhaps a bit of calculation played a role. For a love-relation with the son of the head of the house could have advantages, especially if that relation had brought about fruitful results. She attempted to seduce Fernando. But he rebuffed her.

Speculation enters in here because of the absence of precise details. Some say that Fernando's sexual crisis lasted for several days. Others think that it lasted until his twentieth year, when he began the study of theology. The idea that Fernando/Anthony should have to undergo sexual temptation and even a sexual crisis would not have been shocking for mediaeval hagiography. The legends and biographies of the saints of that period frequently report severe temptations of this sort. Such was the case with Francis, and with Thomas of Aquinas whose own mother sent a naked woman into his room in order to dissuade her son from entering the Dominican Order.

Apparently the mediaeval hagiographers believed that the saints were, above all, also — or only — human beings in whom the general human inclinations could be seen, even in the area of sexuality. It was not customary at that time to be silent about such matters even though one might not have gone into them in great detail.

Today we are inclined to ask: Who appeals to us more? A "saint" who went through life untouched by all human impulses and by the possibility of less noble concerns; or a person who has experienced many basic temptations of body and soul, but who, nevertheless, has walked the road of his or her Christian vocation faithfully? This intermezzo in the life of St. Anthony allows us to see that he was not a man devoid of human passions who walked only on the "high paths." Indeed, he was called to sanctity, but in the fullness of his human reality.

It may be an echo of his youthful experience when Anthony later said: "If we do not resist the evil of debauchery, all our other good intentions will be nipped in the bud . . . Wherever there is excess of riches and pleasure, there dwells the leprosy of the vices. These live in people who are luke-warm and given to idleness. But before it sinks into debauchery, the heart lifts itself up in the spirit of pride which is the beginning of every sin."

In the Cloister of São Vicente de Fora

In 1210, Fernando's life took a decisive turn. He requested admission into the order of the Augustinian canons at the cloister of São Vicente de Fora, (so named because it was "outside the walls of the city.") His parents and other relatives and acquaintances did not make this step easy. Why throw away the chances of a great career? It was not necessary to throw away everything and enter a cloister in order to be faithful to the demands of the Christian life. But Fernando had heard his call and remained firm in his decision.

The cloister of São Vicente was a royal foundation and was richly endowed by King Alfonso. Anyone who lived there enjoyed a secure existence. But soon after Fernando's entrance there, the cloister became involved in conflicts between the church and the king. The peace which Fernando had sought was not to be found. But aside from this, he found himself disturbed in his spiritual endeavors and in his concentration on the studies which were to prepare him for the priesthood. The canons showed great respect for him. And they raised no objections when their younger colleague was visited frequently by relatives, acquaintances, and people his own age who were involved in politics.

While the canons encouraged this as a way of developing more influential relationships, it disturbed Fernando since he wished to be able to develop in peace, especially during the time when he was preparing for the priesthood. So, after two years, he asked his superiors for permission to go to the mother-cloister of Santa Cruz, about 120 miles away in Coimbra. The prior, Don Gonzales, finally gave him permission, even if not gladly.

Canon in Coimbra

At that time, Coimbra was the capital city of the kingdom of Portugal and the seat of the bishop Coimbra also had a fine reputation as a center of studies. Certainly, the world-renowned University of Coimbra did not yet exist during the lifetime of the Saint. It was founded later, in 1307. But the studies of the Augustinians had a good reputation even earlier. This was much to the credit of Canons Raymond and John, both of whom had studied at the University of Paris and had received the Master's degree.

The cloister of Santa Cruz was founded in 1134 by St. Theotonius and had been richly endowed by the Portuguese kings. By the time Fernando arrived there, it had grown to be a vast establishment numbering about sixty members. The library was well-equipped. Naturally, the works of Augustine, the founder of the Order were there. But the works of Ambrose, Bede the Venerable, Gregory the Great, Isidore of Seville were also represented as well as the profane disciplines of the age.

From his later writings it is possible to conclude that Fernando took advantage of the opportunities for study available at Santa Cruz with great intensity. Certainly he had no way of knowing that in his later life he would be actively involved in the conflicts between the church and the heretical teachings of that age. But he was prepared when the challenge came. He possessed an unusually good memory which would later compensate for the lack of books. In study and meditation, he turned himself above all to the Holy Scriptures, especially to the Gospel, which he sought to translate into his life. Pope Gregory IX later called him the "Ark of the Testament," and "Repository of Holy Scripture"; and when he was raised to the status of Doctor of the Church in 1946, Pope Pius XII gave him the title: "Teacher of the Gospel."

Even Coimbra Was no Oasis of Rest

Fernando made his way to Coimbra so that he could concentrate on his vocation without disturbance. But even there in Coimbra the unrest of political struggles caught up with him. There had been discord between the king and the bishops from 1208 onward, and it became ever more intense. The issue was that of the independence of the church from worldly power. The king went so far as to appoint the superiors of the monasteries. The members of the nobility also attempted to strengthen their influence over the church and the monasteries. By means of favors, privileges, and economic arrangements, they attempted to make the dignitaries of the church dependent on them; and many in the church accommodated themselves to this all too willingly, much to the detriment of the independence of the ecclesiastical institutions.

The situation had become so bad that Pope Honorius III felt forced to intervene. This was in 1220, the same year in which Anthony had left the monastery of the canons in Coimbra in order to find a new direction among the followers of St. Francis. The pope expressed his concern with great clarity: "Almost all go their own individual ways and follow only their own interests. To their own loss, they excuse themselves from the banquet of the eternal King. As in ancient Sodom, even priests speak openly of their sins from the altar and thus become a scandal and an occasion for the ruin of the faithful. There is no one who places himself like a wall of protection before the house of God."

Even John, the prior of Santa Cruz, must have felt himself hit by these reproaches of the pope; for he had squandered the possessions of the monastery, living in such a worldly manner himself that he could no longer exercise care for the discipline and order of the monastery. Thus the Augustinian canons themselves were divided by conflict and party strife. Since honesty and absolute consistency were principles of his life, Fernando could not remain neutral. He had to turn against the practises of his prior. He had made the move from Lisbon to Coimbra with the expectation of finding an orderly situation in the monastery of Santa Cruz. But he found himself thrown into poor circumstances. This disappointment may have been a factor in his decision when, several years later, he joined the friars.

The evil of this situation, which was present not only in Santa Cruz, may have been what the Saint had in mind when he later wrote: "The superior is called the father of the house because the subject comes to him as a son into the house of a father in order to find protection from the attack of carnal desires, from the storm of devilish temptations, and from the pervasive passion to strive for earthly possessions."

But the reality was quite different, as even Anthony

indicates: "There is no fair, and no worldly or ecclesiastical tribunal, where monks and religious are not found. They buy and sell; they build and tear down, changing squares into circles. They offer patronage to the opposed parties in law suits, and then fight before the judges, calling on advocates and lawyers as needed. They bring in witnesses who are ready to take oaths concerning unimportant, frivolous, and idle matters. Tell me, you blind members of religious orders, whether you have found in the prophets or in the Gospels of Christ, or in the letters of Saint Benedict or of Augustine such controversies and deceits, or such outcries and protests for the sake of passing, earthly goods."

Marvelous Events in Santa Cruz

Later legends could not depict this time in Santa Cruz simply as a time of darkness caused by human weakness. For the very darkness was a fitting background against which the later wonder-worker could be placed in sharp relief. So the legends tell of a sick colleague in the monastery who was thought to be possessed by a demon. All attempts to calm him had failed. Fernando succeeded with utter simplicity. He covered the troubled man with his capuche, and the man was healed. The Saint's power of exorcism by virtue of which he would later be called on as the great foe of evil spirits was clearly manifest already this early in his life.

The second miraculous tale from this period relates to the personal piety of Fernando, to whom God came near in an unusual way. One day Fernando was appointed to clean the floors. It was precisely the time at which the holy Mass was being celebrated in the church. When the bell signalling the consecration rang, Fernando knelt on the spot where he was in order to worship. In a miraculous way, the walls opened and allowed him to view the holy host elevated after the consecration. Thus, he was able to worship the All Holy with a direct, visual contact.

This account reflects with great exactness a practise of eucharistic piety that was wide-spread at the time. Eucharistic piety had often been so severely reduced that a unique value was placed on the fact that one could see and adore the host elevated after the consecration. Even students of theology frequently came into the church only after the signal for the consecration, adored the elevated host, and then left again.

In the fourth Lateran Council of 1215, the church attempted to change the direction of this impoverished eucharistic piety. This Council required attendance at the entire sacrifice of the Mass at least on Sundays and holy days, and the reception of the holy Eucharist at least once a year, namely, in the Paschal season. St. Francis of Assisi, St. Clare, and St. Anthony in his own way, all took up this concern of the church in an active way. They worked much and accomplished much in restoring life to eucharistic piety.

II.
FERNANDO BECOMES
A FRANCISCAN

The desire to be freed of these unfortunate circumstances may well have played a role in Fernando's departure from Santa Cruz in 1220. On the other hand, the years spent there had given him much. The possibility of studying theology, which he took up eagerly, enriched his faith-life, led to growth in science, and enabled him to mature in wisdom. He had received an excellent preparation for his later work, for which he must have been very grateful. In view of his dynamic character, it might be assumed that, by the time he entered the young Order of the Franciscans, Santa Cruz had become too narrow a place for him to live in. This young Order was consistent in its focus on the Gospel of Jesus Christ. It was also concerned with the needs of the poor and included in its program the mission among non-Christians. All this appealed to Fernando, who needed wide spaces to work out his personal service for God's Kingdom.

The Franciscans Come to Portugal

The religious movement that emanated from St. Francis was not ten years old when it reached Portugal in 1217. It had spread almost like an explosion throughout Europe and to the Near East. People were impressed with these religious who attempted to live the Gospel consistently and without pretensions, who spread peace in the human family and who were simple brothers to all. Their style was different from that of the monks of the older orders. Their open and natural immediacy to God and to other people drew many to follow the same way.

People looked at the Franciscans with curiosity wherever they went, and many even considered them to be heretics. But their simple and humble style soon drew the confidence of the simple people and even of the nobles. In Coimbra, Queen Urraca gave them a chapel dedicated to St. Anthony the Hermit which was located in an olive grove. Therefore, this house of the Franciscans was known as "Santo Antonio dos Olivas." Through the assistance of Sancia, the sister of the king, the brothers of St. Francis obtained a house in Lisbon, or more precisely, in Alenquer.

The Sequence formerly sung on the Feast of St. Francis said about the religious movement that took its origin from him: "A new Order, a new life arise; one of which the world had not heard up to that time." The most common term to describe the person and work of Francis was the word "new." Indeed, when the brothers of St. Francis arrived and remained in the immediate neighborhood, the style of the Franciscans would have been experienced as something new in the world of religious orders at Santa Cruz in Coimbra, and also by Fernando.

These were men who did not stand out because of theological or secular kowledge, nor did they give polished sermons in order to impress others. They lived according to the words of their Rule: "All the brothers should preach through their works." And the sermon of their life was that they lived the Holy Gospel without compromise, and that they understood their own mission to the world in the very words with which Jesus had sent the Apostles into the world (Cfr. Mt 10:5-15). Certainly they preached with simple but impressive words that the Kingdom of God was near. But, above all, it was their life that showed others what the Kingdom of God meant concretely: To be lovingly concerned with those who had been hit with the suffering of the world, to exorcize the demonic from the world, to live with others in poverty and without pretensions, and to spread the peace of God.

Without doubt, once he had encountered this new way of living the ancient and eternally valid Gospel, a young man like Fernando, who was seeking to live an authentic life, would have been moved to reflect about the meaning of this new way of life. But this was only the first impulse which prepared him for the truly decisive step. The second impulse came from the brothers of St. Francis as well.

The Call of the Martyrs

In 1219, a group of friars who had expressed their readiness to undertake a mission among the Saracens had been sent out on their mission by Francis. Brothers Berard, Peter, Otto, Adjutus, and Accursius arrived in Coimbra on their journey to the mission area. There they found the support of the Queen. From there they took a ship to Seville which, at that time, was ruled by the Saracens. One has to ask which motive was stronger in them: the desire to win the Mohammedans to the Christian faith, or the desire for martyrdom.

This desire for martyrdom is mentioned in most of the biographies of the saints of that time, even in the case of Francis. In any event, the five Franciscans preached the Christian faith to the Mohemmedans so aggressively and condemned Mohammed and his followers so sharply that the harshest reactions were inevitable.

The were condemned to death in Seville but were then pardoned and expelled from the territory. They did not give up, however, but travelled to Morocco where they found the support of Peter, the brother of the Portuguese King, Alfonso II. This Peter was an unusual person. He had quarrelled with his royal brother and had gone into the service of the Caliph of Morocco, but he had not abjured his Christian faith.

Soon the inevitable happened. The five friars were arrested again and were ill-treated. Peter was able to free them; but in their determination to achieve martyrdom, these friars again attacked the Islamic faith in public and were beheaded for this on January 16, 1220. Their patron, Peter, procured their bodies secretly and had them sent to Coimbra. Since the house of the friars in Coimbra was far too small to serve as the burial place for the five new martyrs, the cloister of Santa Cruz was chosen for that purpose. It is possible that Peter wished in this way to defy his brother, the king. For Santa Cruz was the burial site of the Portuguese kings. After this spectacular action, Peter could no longer remain in Morocco and soon left.

Fernando, who had already been deeply moved by the Franciscan way of life, and who certainly knew about the adventure of these proto-martyrs of the Franciscan Order, now stood at their very graves. These men who had been slain for their faith summoned him to the same path. The canons of Santa Cruz would soon discover that the gift of the bodies of the five martyrs would be a costly gift for them. For now Fernando, who was greatly respected and full of promise, came with the request that he be allowed to transfer to the brothers of St. Francis.

Fernando Changes Orders and Becomes Anthony

It was not easy to receive the approval of the prior and of the community for the transfer to another order. For, like many monasteries and orders at that time, Santa Cruz had received a papal privilege by reason of which no member of the community could leave the cloister without permission, and no one could be accepted by another order without written permission, and any such transfer must be a change to a stricter order.

It was precisely the last condition that must have appeared to be a judgment on their life-style and a bitter pill for the community of canons. But, in the end, Fernando received the permission he had requested. It is reported that one of the canons said farewell to Fernando with the following words, no doubt intended with irony: "Go now, go. Now finally you can become a saint." Whether or not these words were actually spoken, they could well express the feelings of the convent of canons when one of their members left them to join a "stricter order." Fernando is said to have answered: "Should you ever hear that I have become a saint, then praise the Lord God."

When Fernando transferred to the Order of Franciscan friars in the summer of 1220, the Order had already been organized into provinces since 1217. The leaders of the provinces, called "minister" or "servant," were responsible for the reception of new members. At that time, Portugal belonged to the Spanish province of Santiago, whose provincial was John Parenti. After the death of St. Francis, John would be elected to take his place as minister general.

The house of the friars at Coimbra had Anthony the Hermit as its patron. And Fernando took his name. At that time, it was not the practise that all those entering the Order would be given a new name. When that happened, it was by the free decision of the person involved. Many biographies of Anthony, among them the very oldest — the *Legenda Assidua* — claim that Anthony changed his name so that his relatives and acquaintances would not be able to find him. He wished to remain unknown in his new situation.

Was this really the reason? Anyone who really searched for his new whereabouts could easily discover his new "address" from the canons of Santa Cruz. It would not have been difficult, therefore, to find him under his new name.

Fernando could well have taken the new name "Anthony" as a sign of an entirely new beginning in the sense of the text of Scripture that speaks of putting off the old man and putting on the new man (Cfr. Eph 4:22-23), or in the very radical sense of dying to a new life. He may have thought of this radically new beginning when he wrote later in his sermons:

> "Anyone who wishes to enter a monastery or order in order to do penance thereby enters a tomb. And when he sees the great stone at the entrance to the tomb, that is, the difficulties of life in the order, he will say: Who will remove the stone from the entrance for us? The great stone is the difficulty met with at the entrance . . . But one who loves finds nothing to be difficult."

At the time when Anthony joined the friars in the summer of 1220, it was not necesssary to make a novitiate in the new Order. Therefore, he was able to make his profession immediately. It was only on September 22, 1220, that Pope Honorius III published the regulation that required a novitiate of one year in the Order of St. Francis before the profession of vows. Francis accepted this regulation into the Rule of the Order which dates back to 1221.

As Soon as Possible to Morocco

Immediately after his entrance into the Franciscan Order, Anthony did something not generally welcomed by religious superiors in the case of new members. He approached his superiors with clear ideals as to how his life should go in the future. He asked for permission to go as a missionary to Morocco. Without doubt the example of the five martyrs of Morocco called him.

Anthony's request was not the mere posturing of a young man determined to take an aggressive line in setting out his own path of self-realization. Rather, he was making use of a custom that would find its textual form in the Rule of 1221 but which, no doubt, was in force even before that. The Rule says: "Any of the brothers who wishes to go among the Saracens and other unbelievers may go with the permission of his minister and servant. (Francis called the leaders of his brotherhood 'ministers' or 'servants.') And the minister should give them permission and should not oppose them if he sees that they are fit to be sent. For he shall have to give an account of it to the Lord if he acts inadvisedly in this or in other matters."

Anthony Finds Out: "Not in This Way!"

Anthony received permission from his provincial. Thus, toward the end of the year 1220, he set out on the way to his mission and to the desired goal accompanied by a brother named Philip. "But the Almighty withstood him to the face," says the *Legenda Assidua*, the oldest account of the life of the Saint. God said to him: "Not in this way!" He had an experience similar to that which Paul had when he arrived at the shore of Asia Minor on a missionary journey, wishing to go inland to take up his missionary work. "The Spirit of Jesus did not allow them," says the Acts of the Apostles (16:7). Paul was to go to Europe, contrary to his original intention. He also had an experience that let him know he was not to do things in this way.

But Anthony's experience was very different from that of Paul. Anthony had hardly arrived in Morocco when he fell sick. And the feverish sickness would not let up. It kept him in bed for the whole of the winter and into the spring of 1221. Someone was convinced that the climate of Morocco was unfavorable for his recovery and explained to the sick man that it would be better to return to the climate of his homeland in order to regain his full strength. He agreed and boarded a ship that was to take him back home. Since according to the direction of St. Francis, fraternal love would not want to leave a sick person alone, a confrere accompanied him. But again came the sign: "Not in this way." Even though the voyage home had been delayed until the spring when one would not have to reckon so strongly with winter storms, still a terrible storm broke out. Instead of moving toward Spain and Portugal, the ship was forced in the opposite direction and was eventually driven to Sicily.

After severe trials on this stormy voyage, Anthony was able to land on the east coast of Sicily where the friars of the house at Messina received him with love and helped him to regain his strength. He had time for reflection. He had experienced that his life was not to go in this way; and in faith, he accepted this as a sign from God. But what did God wish him to do? He was ready to entrust himself in obedience to the will of God and waited for God's direction.

The Pentecost Chapter of the Friars at the Portiuncula in 1221

The general chapter of the Order was set for the Feast of Pentecost at the Portiuncula chapel on the plain below Assisi. Together with the other brothers, Anthony made his way there. At that time, general chapters were not gatherings of the leaders of the Order. Anyone who desired could come. One serious reason for Anthony to go to the chapter could well have been his desire to meet or at least to see Francis. At the beginning of Francis' new way, the Portiuncula chapel had been restored by his own hand. It was here that he had received the basic instructions for his life from the Gospel on the feast of St. Matthias. It was the missionary mandate of Jesus to his disciples that had moved him deeply. Francis had chosen this chapel as the

Mother-church of his brotherhood where the brothers met regularly on the Feast of Pentecost for general chapters.

We are well-informed concerning the Feast of Pentecost of the year 1221, since Brother Jordan of Giano gave a somewhat detailed report of the chapter in his chronicle. About three thousand novices and professed brothers took part in it. Let us simply accept this number as it is recorded. It is not possible for us to calculate exactly how many were really there. Regardless of the exact number, the band of brothers had become very large. What a mighty pilgrimage took place in most of Europe whenever the brothers held their chapter! In large numbers, they left the place where they lived and worked simply to meet once again as brothers, gathering "to reflect on things that pertain to God"; for this was what Francis had seen as the purpose of such chapter-gatherings. This witness of brotherliness must have made a very deep impression on their contemporaries.

Certainly since such large numbers caused problems for the conducting of these chapters, particulary the chapter of 1221, it became necessary to take the large number into account. The old practise according to which all the brothers, even the novices, could take part in the general chapter was abrogated later, and the general chapters became practically chapters of the leaders of the Order. One may certainly regret this development. But was it really the case that the leaders — known as "servants of the others" — really wished to establish themselves as superiors?

It is certain that in any vote taken among three thousand brothers, the provincial leaders would have been a hopeless minority. But we must evaluate this reduction of chapter participants without modern emotions. At that time, the basic concern would have been the serious problems that such large numbers would have involved for running a general chapter. For it was not simply a matter of a simple, brotherly gathering with no other particular purpose. A general chapter also had to make decisions concerning the direction that the Order should take for the future. And at the general chapter of 1221, the issue was the text of a Rule for the Order which was to be observed by all. This was not simply a case of Francis' presenting the text of the Rule to the brothers and demanding their acceptance of it. As a letter to an unknown superior of the Order proves, Francis wished the collaboration of his brothers in the writing of the text of the Rule, and had asked directly for this.

In 1221, it would not have been an easy task to run a general chapter with three thousand brothers. Even today, despite all the modern technological instruments available, this would involve great difficulties. How could anyone succeed with it at that time?

Because of the friars' simple life-style, the question of lodging would have been relatively easy to solve. The brothers simply built huts for themselves out of the reeds that grow so commonly in Italy, and covered them with straw. According to the account of Brother Jordan of Giano, the meals were taken at three hundred and twenty tables which "were set up in a certain order." And certainly, the local population felt honored that their region had become a sort of center for friars who were spread widely throughout Europe. They had provided food so generously that after the seven days of the chapter, the brothers had to be asked to remain two days longer in order to use up all the provisions.

How Did Anthony Experience St. Francis?

Francis had spent about one year in the Orient. After his return, at the Pentecost chapter at the Portiuncula on May 17, 1220, he had appointed Brother Peter Cathanii as his vicar. After Peter's death on May 10, 1221, Francis appointed Brother Elias of Cortona to this office. Francis delegated to his vicars all the powers that were necessary for the administration of the Order. While he remained the head of the Order, he withdrew from the more administrative tasks. This became very clear at the chapter of 1221. While Cardinal Rainer Capocci presided at the gathering, everything that pertained to the organization and running of the chapter lay firmly in the hands of Brother Elias. Francis sat humbly on the floor next to him. But whenever he sensed that a spiritual word was necessary to clarify something in the discussions and business affairs, he made this known to Elias by pulling on his habit. Elias would then tell the chapter-assembly: "Brothers, the brother would like to say something to you." And then Francis spoke. He was referred to simply as "the brother."

In Francis and Elias, Anthony experienced two different types, or perhaps we could say two dimensions, of power. Each of these types of power is important in its own way for the brotherhood of the Order, but they must be kept in their proper relation to each other. On the one side there was the charism of spirituality; on the other side there was the organizational, institutional dimension. These powers must complement each other. At the chpater of 1221, this complementary relation was realized in a healthy way.

We do not know whether Anthony and Francis actually met in person at this chapter, but is is highly unlikely that they would have. Anthony must have been very reserved during the days of the chapter, and apparently he did not talk even in private about his noble background or about his outstanding theological education. Now that God had cut through his previous plans, he did not push himself forward for particular tasks. He remained unknown.

No One Reckoned with Anthony

At the end of the chapter, the brothers were divided among the different provinces in accordance with the tasks of the Order. And Anthony was almost left with no place to go. None of the provincial ministers set much store in having him for his own province. No one recognized as yet what a gift had been given to the Order in the person of this young brother. So Anthony approached Brother Gratian, the provincial of the upper Italian province of the Romagna, and asked him to approach Francis and Brother Elias with the request that he be sent to the province of the Romagna. And so it came about that Brother Gratian took him with him to his province.

At his request, Anthony was assigned to the little hermitage of Monte Paolo, situated near Forli, between Rimini and Bologna. This hermitage was located on a hill, four-hundred meters above sea-level. In good weather, it was possible to view the sea to the east. There was a small church on the spot, some simple cells, and a small garden. It was a typical Franciscan hermitage of the kind that Francis himself had liked.

In the Seclusion of Monte Paolo

From the very beginning, the Order of St. Francis was marked by a clear tendency toward the life of seclusion and contemplation. Even after Francis had decided that he and his brothers would give themselves to the work of the apostolic life, there always remained the possibility for the friars to withdraw to a hermitage for a shorter or longer period of time in order to devote themselves entirely to contemplation. This alternative to the active, apostolic life was, so to say, "legalized" by Francis in as far as he wrote a "Rule for Hermitages." It is clear from this Rule that Francis did not understand the hermitage to mean that an individual brother would live there entirely by himself. Even here, Francis wanted to have a small community with three or four brothers.

In Monte Paolo, Anthony found what he had sought and needed earlier. Here, in undisturbed seclusion, prayer, contemplation, and penance, he had the opportunity to find his way to himself and to God, and — in the presence of God — to integrate into his life all those things which had happened to him: his life as an Augustinian canon, his transfer to the Franciscans, the attempt to take up missionary work in Morocco, the frustration of all his plans. It had been necessary for him to experience clearly the way he was not to follow. Now he awaited a sign from God to indicate what he ought to do in the future. In order to be totally undisturbed, he withdrew into a cave. In his great zeal for penance, he must have gone to extremes, for once when the bell rang to call the brothers together, he collapsed out of weakness.

But he began to realize that he ought to place his abilities at the service of his brothers and not simply wear himself out with penance. So he told the guardian of the house that he would like to share fully in the work and services of the community. He took over the task of washing the dishes and cleaning the floor.

Priestly Ordination in Forli

What did God desire of him at this stage? It almost sounds like an answer to this when he later said: "The saints are like the stars. Through his providence, Christ keeps them hidden so that they do not shine openly even though they would like to. Yet they are always ready to exchange the quiet of contemplation for the works of mercy as soon as they sense the call of Christ in their hearts."

The moment finally came when God showed him to what he was truly being called. He had been at Monte Paolo for about a year when the provincial summoned a number of brothers from different houses to come to Forli. Anthony was among them. They were to be ordained to the priesthood by Bishop Ricciardellus Belmonti. This was in the summer of 1222.

At this point a controversial question arises: Did Anthony receive ordination to the priesthood in the summer of 1222 in Forli, or had he already been ordained in Coimbra? The oldest source for the life of Anthony, the *Legenda Assidua* (which goes back to 1232, one year after his death), has this to say concerning the brothers who were called to Forli for ordination at that time: "Among them was Anthony." The claim that Anthony had already been ordained in Coimbra is not found until 1293 in the "Vita S. Antonii" written by Peter Raymond of San Romano. In such cases, one ought to give the benefit of the doubt to the older source.

Another reason can be given in favor of the year 1222. According to the church law of the time, it was required that a candidate for ordination should have completed his thirtieth year. It was only in cases of genuine necessity that a man could be ordained at the age of twenty-five. Such a necessity could be envisioned at Monte Paolo because of the lack of priests, but not at Coimbra. But without the statement of the *Legenda Assidua*, we could come to no absolutely certain conclusion that Anthony was ordained in 1222. This is connected with the fact that we are not certain about the precise date of his birth. If he was born in 1195, then he would have been twenty-five years old when he left the canons. But if he was born in 1188, then he would have been already thirty-two years old; in which case, he could have been ordained to the priesthood with no difficulty. But many factors speak against the possibility that Anthony was already a priest when he arrived at Monte Paolo. Only if he were not a priest could he have really remained "undiscovered" for a year. Had he been a priest already, his qualities would certainly have been discovered. For, even though a sermon was not always given at Mass at that time, still he would have offered some personal words in an address or homily at the Eucharistic celebration at least from time to time.

Whatever the case may have been, at the ordination at Forli the puzzle was solved. Some Dominicans had received ordination as well. After the celebration, the participants gathered for a common meal in the Dominican cloister. The provincial of the Franciscans suggested that, instead of the table reading, one of the Dominicans should give a sermon. Now, it is indeed a challenge to give a sermon with no preparation, especially when the "competition" is present in the form of another order. Hence, no one was willing to take on the task for fear of making a fool of himself. Then the provincial turned to Anthony and urged him to give a sermon. He should simply say what the Holy Spirit moved him to say. Perhaps the provincial was thinking that if Anthony should make a fool of himself, it would be possible to say: "Well, yes. This is the one who washes the dishes and cleans the floor for us. We should not expect much."

Then Anthony began his sermon, honestly, simply, and without artifice as is possible only for a person of superior quality. The longer he spoke, the more strongly his listeners fell under his spell. Now the unexpected richness of his learning and the sure knowledge of the Word of God with which he explained the mysteries of faith became clear. Although not planned by him, this moment marked the turn in his life to his real task.

He had sought public ministry when he decided on his missonary work in Morocco. But God had led him to the life of quiet contemplation in seclusion so that he could mature for that moment in which God's will would become clear. That moment had arrived at the ordination at Forli. Anthony was appointed to the work of the apostolate and of preaching.

III.
APOSTOLIC WORK IN UPPER ITALY

Did the provincial of the Romagna assign the Saint to the preaching apostolate immediately after the discovery of his ability? He would have had the jurisdiction to do so. Provisions were made for such a case by the "Regula non bullata" which had been in effect since the end of 1221: "None of the brothers shall preach contrary to the procedure and regulations of the holy church, and unless permission has been granted him by his minister. And the minister shall be on guard not to grant permission to anyone inadvisedly." Seldom has this prescription of the Rule been as carefully observd as in the case of St. Anthony, both from the side of the provincial and from that of Anthony himself.

In view of the extent of the assignment, it is entirely possible that the provincial of the Romagna made the decision together with the provincial chapter, particularly since the territory assigned to Anthony practically corresponded with the provincial territory of the Romagna. That particular provincial chapter took place on September 29, 1222. According to the Rule in effect at that time: "Every year each minister can come together with his brothers wherever it pleases them, on the feast of St. Michael the Archangel, in order to treat those things which pertain to God."

As we have already noted, the preaching commission given to St. Anthony extended to the entire territory of the

Franciscan Province of the Romagna. This included not only the actual land called "Romagna," but Lombardy, Emilia, and the territory around Venice, Friuli, and Genoa. Practically, this was all of upper Italy. This territory was the scene of the first period of the Saint's preaching, which extended from 1222 to 1224.

The Religious Situation

It is important to understand the religious background for the apostolic preaching activity of the Saint. The major problem in the church at that time was not that great numbers of people had become areligious and were uninterested in hearing the message of Christ; in a truly tragic sense, the case was just the opposite. The twelfth and thirteenth centuries were marked by a wide-spread religious movement. At least in part, this was a result of the Crusades. By itself, the idea of winning the holy places in Palestine would have brought greater attention to the earthly life of Jesus. But the Crusaders had actually experienced the earth and the paths on which our Lord had walked.

Within the spiritual realm of this religious movement the new ideal of the "Following of Christ" had arisen. Certainly this piety remained conscious of the fact that Jesus Christ, the eternal Son of God, reigned in the glory of the trinitarian life of God. But now attention shifted emphatically to the human existence of the Son of God. It was recognized that the incarnate Son of God had walked our human paths, and that his footprints were on our earth. We human beings were able to follow him in these paths.

The Waldensians and Other "Evangelical" Groups

The impulse for this religious movement came not "from above," from the hierarchy of the church, but "from below," and for the most part from people who were untrained in theology. It was strongly rooted in the emerging middle class. These were people who had discovered the Gospel and wished to live it in total poverty, in the sense of Jesus' call to discipleship. One such man was Peter Waldo. He was a wealthy merchant of Lyons who took seriously and personally the words of Jesus to the rich, young man. He sold all his possessions and distributed the money to the poor. Since he knew no Latin, he had the Gospel translated into his mother-tongue. Many others did as he had done. They gathered in like-minded groups, read the Gospel, and discussed how they might live their lives in its light. Bishops were shocked at this and turned to Pope Innocent III. What were they to do in this situation where lay persons were reading the Gospel in their own tongue and meditating on it together? The pope answered that they should let the people have their way. The bishops should only take care that the translations of the Scriptures contained no errors that would lead to false understandings.

The ideal of these groups was to live in the manner of Christ and the Apostles just as the Gospel describes it. But they did not wish to be merely passive recipients of the Gospel. Interested in active engagement in apostolic work, they wanted to proclaim the Gospel to others together with the summons to penance and conversion. At this point, a tragic conflict arose. The church wished to allow only the clergy to preach, and not the laity. A compromise was attempted with Peter Waldo. Rome allowed him and his followers to preach as lay persons when they were invited and asked to do so by the priests. Even though this agreement could have prevented a lot of trouble, the priests did not agree to it.

So it happened that these groups, which had become so alert to the Gospel, began to preach without ecclessiastical permission. As lay people, they were not educated in matters of dogma. As a result, their sermons did not always agree with the teaching of the church. And since they had now fallen into a conflict with the clergy, they attacked the clergy without mercy in their sermons. On the other hand, the disreputable life-style of many of the clergy opened itself to the possibiity of such attacks. And it was the clergy who forbade the right of preaching to these committed lay people who wished only to live the life of the Gospel fully.

So it happened that many circles made the claim that the power to preach was not bound to any ecclesiastical commission or to ordination. What is required and suffi-cient for this task is an upright life. In the end, it was claimed that the true church could be found only where the apostolic life was being lived in its fullest. And where no priest could be found who was living the apostolic life, the "good" person — a lay person living in the apostolic life — had the right to administer the sacraments and to preach the word of God. With this, sound church teaching had been abandoned. And so it happened that the church saw unauthorized lay preaching as essentially heretical in nature.

This situation and these experiences with wayward groups of the religious movement certainly played a role when Francis petitioned the pope for the approval of his Rule in 1209. What he desired — "to observe poverty and humility and the Gospel of our Lord, Jesus Christ" — was what so many others had already wished to do. But most of the others had come into conflict with the church with such a fatal regularity that the Roman curia had an almost allergic reaction whenever someone else came with the desire to take the Gospel as a program of life.

This makes it understandable that the Roman curia should at first have been very reserved in its reaction when Francis asked for the confirmation of his way of life which was founded on the Gospel. Many of our contemporaries take almost malicious pleasure in explaining this hesita-tion of the cardinals by saying that the cardinals them-selves did not believe that the Gospel could really be lived. The Roman curia had become that corrupt. It would be more accurate to see the cardinals as people who had been burned in their dealings with various groups of the religious movement.

If, despite all the bitter experiences with all the other groups of the religious movement, Pope Innocent III did give St. Francis the ecclesiastical approval of his Rule, this was because a decisive element was added to the saint's desire "to observe poverty and humility and the Gospel of our Lord, Jesus Christ," namely, the readiness to live "always submissive and prostrate at the feet of this holy church, standing firmly in the Catholic faith." This formulation comes from the Rule of 1223. But the attitude toward the church was present from the beginning. Had that not been the case, it would have been impossible for the Franciscan brotherhood to exist within the church.

Pope Innocent III had recognized the danger that the widespread religious movement with its new concentration on the following of Christ could develop outside the church and could even be turned against it. By giving ecclesiastical approval to Francis and his community, he provided a legal place within the church for this new ideal of the Christian life. For Francis bore within himself all the religious yearnings of his time. But he wished to realize them within the church. With this came the possibility of bringing the alienated people back to the church. Through Francis and his brothers — and also through Dominic and his new Order — the church would be able to show that it was possible to follow the way of Christ as strictly and as fully as the other groups wished to do, and to do this while remaining fully within the context of the Catholic church. Apostolic work was carried out in these new Orders of the church not only by teaching but by their life-style itself.

The Cathari

The so-called Cathari were even more dangerous than the groups of the religious movement just discussed, who after all, were fundamentally Christian, even if they did not always wish to remain within the church. It is from the name of the Cathari that the German word for "heretic" is derived, namely, "Ketzer." They held the view that all material, earthly reality was fundamentally corrupt and evil because it was created by an evil god. It was particularly in sexual production of life that they saw the real sin. Anyone who desired to be "pure" would have to avoid all contact with anything that came into existence through sexual procreation. For this reason, they forbade the use of those foods whose enjoyment would make one unclean. This concerned particularly the use of meat, while fish was seen as "pure." As we shall see, this precise point would play a role in the life of St. Anthony.

The Cathari rejected all sacraments since these involved material things: bread, wine, oil, etc. And since, in their view, it was inconceivable that the spiritual nature of the Word could have united itself with an earthly body, they denied that Christ had been truly human. The Redeemer had assumed only an apparent body; sufferings had been only apparent and not real.

The doctrines of the Cathari were not Christian, but people streamed to them in large numbers. Simple people who could not distinguish between doctrine and life saw something good here since the Cathari lived in a strict and radical style, in a style of self-denial and renunciation, and were ready even to undergo death for their convictions.

Preaching Through Works

This was the situation into which Anthony was sent with a commission to take up the task of apostolic, missionary preaching. It was clear to him from the start that even the most beautiful words in a sermon could not convert anyone if the preacher did not consistently live what he preached to others. In his own case, the people sensed that the teaching of his sermons was lived in his life, where it could be seen with exemplary clarity. It was just as Francis had demanded in his Rule of 1221: "All the brothers should preach by their deeds."

A preacher who stood behind his words with his own life had the right to point out mistaken behavior to people of all states, professions, and age groups clearly, precisely, and without compromise in order to lead them to conversion, to penance, and to God's salvation. This style was successful, as proved by the crowds that came to the sacrament of penance after his sermons. Anthony himself had emphasized this point strongly in his admonitions to preachers: "The preacher speaks with two lips: with his life and with his good reputation. These two lips should safeguard his knowledge so that he might show to his neighbor all that he knows and preaches, both through his upright life and through his knowledge. The art of a fruitful sermon flows from these two lips." "The preacher must possess science and knowledge. Above all, he should be able to distinguish what, when, and to whom he is preaching. Then he should be able to recognize whether he himself lives what he preaches to others." The Saint had apparently also had the experience that a preacher who feels obliged by the truth and calls things by their name does not find enthusiastic agreement from all. This could happen particularly when social problems were exposed to the light of God's word without mercy. Anthony did not allow himself to be misled even when he experienced the hatred of many people.

He knew well that not all preachers had the courage to expose injustices publicly. Even though the accounts of his life tell of the great enthusiasm with which his sermons were received, he knew that there were other reactions as well. And he had certainly experienced them. Otherwise his admonitions to preachers would hardly have been as clear as they seem to be in the following words: "Christ says of himself, 'I am the truth' (Jn 14:6). Anyone who proclaims the truth acknowledges Christ. Anyone who conceals the truth through his preaching denies Christ. Truth awakens hatred. And in order to avoid the hatred of certain people, many hide their mouths in the mantle of silence. If they were to proclaim the truth as it really is, as honesty requires, and as the Holy Scriptures expressly demand, they would, without doubt, experience the hatred of worldly people and would, perhaps, be excluded from their company. But they 'speak in human terms' (1 Cor 3:3) because they are afraid that people will be offended. You blind preachers. Because you are afraid of offending the blind, you yourselves fall into blindness of the heart."

Social Problems Were Attacked Relentlessly

When Anthony speaks about matters that oppress the poor, it becomes clear that his attacks on injustice and social disorders spring not from the desire to gain an enthusiastic reaction, but from an uncompromising honesty that felt obligated only to the Gospel. Those who were hit by his attacks must have cried out in rage and fury when they realized how clearly they were described:

"The accursed usurers become great and strong on the earth. Their teeth are like the teeth of lions. The lion is distinguished by two qualities: a neck that will not bend since it is made of but one bone, and an evil-smelling mouth. Similarly, the neck of the usurer is unbending since he neither fears God nor respects his fellow human beings. His mouth smells evil because he puts nothing into it except filthy money and its dirty profit. His teeth are like those of a young lion (Joel 1:6), for he swallows and consumes the property of the poor, the orphans, and the widows."

"Anyone who strangles another person takes from that person both his voice and his life. The poor person's property is his life. As life lives from blood, so the poor person must live from his property. If you take his meager possessions from the poor person, you suck out his life-blood. In doing so, you strangle that person; and in the end, you yourself will be strangled by the devil."

If this is not specific enough, Anthony could become so unmistakably concrete that many people had to know that they had been singled out, even some in ecclesisastical circles. "One who wishes to lord it over others uses gold and silver money as a security at the curia, giving it to porters and notaries, for such people well understand how to milk a cow. They suck out the blood of the poor and lighten the purses of the wealthy and give the money to their nephews and nieces, and often even to their sons and daughters. They write out receipts for the money requested from them, and desire to receive great sums of gold and silver in payment. They strip their fellow human beings of everything, taking even their clothing. Even the people living in the cities are driven to complain, and the souls of those who are oppressed cry out to the Lord. But God leaves nothing unpaid. If they have acted against the light of their better insights, they will lose the light of grace and of the church."

According to the legends, Anthony did not depend only on the power of his words but was able to illustrate what he said by wonderful actions. There was a very wealthy man who had died in Florence. He had been so successful in his money-affairs that he was able to force his will on the government of the city. As his corpse was being brought to the burial, Anthony intervened. He stopped the funeral procession and told the participants that the dead man was not worthy of receiving a Christian burial. Let the corpse be opened, and no heart will be found inside. The heart will be found in the money-box of the deceased. They did as Anthony suggested. Indeed, the heart of the avaricious man was found not in the corpse but with his money.

This very drastic and macabre account is intended

basically to present in graphic clarity what Anthony had said in his sermons. The power of this account can be seen in the fact that the story was told in parish-missions right down to the present century. In essence, it is nothing other than a strong expression of the word of Jesus: "For where your treasure is, there will your heart be also" (Mt 6:21).

The Cathari Attempt to Defame Anthony

In his work, Anthony had to engage vigorously in dispute with the erroneous teachings of the Cathari. He was a difficult opponent who could not be overcome merely by words. Therefore, the Cathari attempted to defame him. Thus, the legend describes how the heretics placed a roasted chicken on the table before the Saint on a Friday and pointed out to him that according to the Gospel, a person is permitted to eat of everything that is placed before him. As Anthony actually began to eat, his opponents secretly summoned the bishop. It was hoped that he himself would be a witness to the fact that Anthony had not observed the current rule of abstinence. By the time the bishop arrived on the scene, Anthony had already eaten the chicken, or at least his portion of the chicken. Only the bones remained. But Anthony knew how to help himself. He made the sign of the cross and changed the "corpus delicti" into fish bones. Now his opponents looked foolish, for not only was it permitted to eat fish on Friday, but fish was a "clean" food even in the eyes of the Cathari.

Apparently here the legend has taken an occurrence from the life of Francis and transferred it to Anthony, changing its meaning in the process. In the original version concerning Francis, the question of Friday abstinence was not the issue. The story was concerned rather with the fact that, for the Cathari, the eating of meat was considered to be "unclean" and sinful whereas fish was considered to be "clean." In the legend of Anthony this point is no longer clearly recognizable. Nonetheless, the evidence of a confrontation with the Cathari can be recognized in relation to both Francis and Anthony.

With respect to the Cathari and their teaching about unclean foods that make a person unclean, Francis included the following statement in the Rule of the Order: "And, according to the holy Gospel, they are free to eat of whatever food is set before them." This regulation should not be seen as a relaxation of a strict style of life. Rather, when viewed against its contemporary background, it is truly a confession of faith.

Difficult Terrain at Rimini

It was especially in Rimini that Anthony encountered the bitter opposition of the Cathari. This is attested to in a number of accounts. It must be remembered that, in the case of Rimini, the bishop had expelled the Cathari from the city already in the year 1180. But the podestà had let them return to the city because of the pressure of the populace, who were fascinated by the severe asceticism of these heretics.

And now a person who would later be given the name "Hammer of heretics" arrives in the city. In an attempt to render him harmless, his opponents invited him to a dinner at which his food had been poisoned. Anthony saw through the evil trick. His enemies maintained that, as a man of God, he should believe the word of Jesus: "If they drink any deadly thing, it will not hurt them" (Mk 16:18). The Saint partook of the food with no harmful effects to his health.

Certainly this miracle-account is intended to depict the evil cynicism of his enemies. But it is a concern of the legend also to show how the words of Sacred Scripture come to concrete expression in the life of the Saint. It is precisely this that so often comes to expression in the ancient accounts of the life of Anthony. Through his sermons, Anthony had come to be known as a theologian with a deep knowledge of the Scriptures. This fact is translated into concrete images by the legends.

Anthony Preaches to the Fish

Another event is associated with Rimini: the sermon to the fish. The account in which this is contained is not among the most reliable. But even if it is not based on an actual occurrence, still it shows well the circumstances in Rimini at the time and sketches an appropriate picture of Anthony. According to the account, Anthony's enemies had gained considerable success in convincing people to boycott his sermons, thus drawing the public away from the preacher. Anthony persisted in carrying out his mission in his own way.

He decided that the Gospel would be preached in Rimini nonetheless. And if the people of this city on the sea were not willing to hear it, he would preach it to those on whom these people depended for their life, namely, the fish. For a spiritual son of St. Francis, this was not an absurd idea. For Francis had seen it as meaningful and even necessary to preach the message of the eternal Word to all creatures that had been created through the eternal Word, including birds, fish, and even the corn-fields. And, as their reactions indicate, the creatures had listened to Francis.

So, Anthony went to the shore of the Adriatic where the river Marechia flowed into the sea. And the fish swarmed in great numbers in order to hear him. Their behavior was very different from what we see among human persons when they gather in great numbers. Among the fish, a good social order was maintained. They gathered before the preacher in rows that were precisely ordered; the smallest were in the front while the larger ones were toward the rear. None stood in the way of the others. And, contrary to their normal need and custom, they kept their heads out of the water for the whole of the sermon. At the end of the sermon, they nodded their heads in thanks and opened their mouths to show that they had accepted the sermon, even though they made no sound since fish have no voice.

This remarkable story very likely provokes a sceptical smile for us today. The famous court-preacher of Vienna in the eighteenth-century, Abraham of Sancta Clara, also expressed scepticism at the concrete details of the sermon to the fish. He depicts the sermon of Anthony in his own way. The beginning goes as follows:

> "When Anthony arrives to preach, he finds the
>   church empty.
> He goes to the river and preaches to the fish:
> They beat the water with their tails, they gleam in
>   the sunshine."

Then he addresses each group: the carp, the pike, the cod, the eels, the sturgeons, the crayfish, and the turtles. Always came the same refrain:

> "No sermon has ever so pleased us."

But in the version of Abraham of Santa Clara, the story of the sermon to the fish ends with the following:

> "When the sermon ended, all turned.
> The pike remained thieves, the eels still loved to
>   have a lot.
> The sermon has pleased them; they remain as they
>   were.
> The crayfish go backwards, the cod remain fat,
> The carp eat a lot and forget the sermon.
> The sermon has pleased them; they remain as they
>   were."

It is quite clear that in his fish-sermon, Abraham of Santa Clara is referring to his own audience, that is, to the people standing around his own pulpit. The "original" fish-sermon of St. Anthony also referred to human persons, even if in an unusual way, namely, as a demonstration of unbelief. Whatever the case may be concerning the historical actualities of this story, in the Middle Ages, wonderful events were treasured; and this story was first told in the Middle Ages. In the Middle Ages, such miracle-accounts spread quickly and contributed greatly to the fame of a particular saint.

Did anyone really think that Anthony had dealt a decisive blow to the Cathari with his sermon to the fish? For among the Cathari, fish were "clean" animals, and were set apart from evil beings. These "clean" animals had accepted Anthony, whereas the "clean" Cathari had categorically rejected him.

The Miracle of the Mule and the Host

Yet another occurrence is associated with Rimini. It clearly expresses the difficulties which Anthony experienced with the Cathari. There was a certain man by the name of Bonillo who had been with the Cathari for more than thirty years and had already reached the level of the "perfect." Being one of the Cathari, he rejected the sacraments of the church, particularly the Sacrament of the Eucharist. Now Anthony, who clearly and emphatically proclaimed the church's teaching about the Eucharist, crossed paths with him:

> "Christ was transfigured on Mount Tabor. This mountain symbolizes the altar on which, similarly, a transfiguration takes place, namely, the change of the substance of bread and wine into the flesh and blood of Jesus. Through this sacrament the light of God enters into the souls of believers."

"Therefore we must firmly believe and confess with our mouth: That body which the Virgin bore, which hung on the cross, which lay in the tomb, rose on the third day, and ascended to the right hand of the Father; this body he has truly offered to his apostles today; this body the church changes daily and distributes to the faithful. When the priest speaks the words: This is my body, the substance of the bread is changed into the body of Christ."

These words, taken from a sermon for Holy Thursday, certainly were not spoken at Rimini. But they clearly represent the precise character of St. Anthony's faith, which stands in complete harmony with the teaching of the church. Therefore, we have placed them in this context.

Recognized as one of the Cathari by the populace and hence as an opponent of Anthony, Bonillo apparently did not want to attack Anthony with words in any sort of public debate. The power of Anthony's words was so great that Bonillo could hardly expect to win in a verbal debate. Therefore, he looked for another way to make Anthony's situation impossible. It seems that he took his cue from Anthony's own preaching when he described the conditions under which he would be ready to believe in the Eucharist. A mule should be denied food for three days. On the fourth day it should be placed between a pile of oats and a consecrated host. Then they would see which way the animal would turn.

A moving drama took place on the fourth day. A throng of very curious people gathered at the piazza. The mule was brought to the spot. A great mound of food was placed before it as Anthony approached the animal with the Holy Sacrament. Then the incomprehensible happened: The hungry animal knelt before the Lord present in the consecrated host and paid no attention at all to the food. That was convincing. Bonillo and many with him were converted to the faith of the church as Anthony had proclaimed it.

Questions About the Miracle of the Mule and the Host

The central point of this account is obviously the surprising conversion of Bonillo. To a later period, this conversion would seem to require some miracle at Rimini on the part of Anthony. And in the sixteenth century, Rimini claimed this miracle for itself by having a chapel built on the place where the miracle is supposed to have happened. Rimini had every reason to lay claim to this miracle by erecting a sacred building, for there was considerable competition among other cities who likewise claimed this as their miracle. In general, this "miracle of the mule" or "miracle of the host" has had a distinctive history.

Neither the oldest legend nor the documents of the canonization-process refer to this miracle. In fact, these sources do not speak of any miracles from the life-time of the Saint. It was only after his death that Anthony became known throughout the world as a wonder-worker. And in the light of the numerous miracles that took place through his intercession after his death, it was concluded that he must have worked miracles during his life as well.

In any case, it is noteworthy that the earliest account of the "miracle of the mule" or the "miracle of the host" makes no reference to Anthony. On the contrary, it attributes the miracle to some priest who is not identified more precisely. It is striking not only that this story occurs in the "Book of Exemplary Deeds of the Friars Minor in the Thirteenth Century" (*Liber exemplorum Fratrum Minorum saeculi XIII*), but also that the author of this book was a Franciscan. Had this author known that his holy colleague, Anthony, was a miracle-worker, he certainly would not have been silent about such a fact that could have contributed to the fame of his Order.

In the year 1300, Rigaldus attributes the miracle to St. Anthony. But he does not specify where it took place. The Legend "Benignitas," written after 1300, designates the place as Toulouse. Around the year 1400, Bartholomew of Pisa places the miracle in Rimini. And in the sixteenth century, Luke Wadding is of the opinion that it took place at Bourges. No doubt, local patriotism played a role in all these cases since, because of the lack of precision in the first account of the miracle, any city could claim the miracle as its own. The same sort of thing happened with other miracle-accounts. The dilemma created by this could later be solved by claiming that Anthony had worked the same miracle several times. Besides, in the Middle Ages there are other instances in the lives of saints where a number of cities claim the same miraculous occurrences as their own.

We can hardly solve this problem today. But if we ask about the significance of all these partly contradictory traditions, they can be seen as a concrete illustration of the unusual impact which the work of the Saint had. For in all the cities named, Anthony had been engaged with people opposed to the Catholic doctrine of the Eucharist. But, even more clearly, these traditions illustrate that the veneration of the Saint was so widespread after his death that different places could compete with each other in this way.

Jesus Christ, True God and True Man

The Cathari denied the true humanity of the Savior. According to their viewpoint, one ought not think that God, who is pure spiritual being, would have assumed a human body capable of death. If Anthony wished to be true to his missionary vocation, he would have to clearly explain the doctrine concerning the one who, though God, assumed a human nature. He would have to do this without so emphasizing the humanity of Jesus Christ that there would be no room left for the divinity, on the one hand; and without allowing his true divinity to stand so strongly in the foreground that his true humanity would not be sufficiently accounted for, on the other hand. The perpetual problem of Christology consists in the fact that one or the other side is overemphasized and a true balance between them is not achieved. Statements of the Saint that have come down to us concerning this matter of the Christian faith date from a later period of his life. But from these statements, we can draw out the sort of Christology which he would have expressed in his sermons from the beginning.

"Because Adam did not wish to serve the Lord in Paradise (Jer 2:20), therefore the Lord assumed the form of a servant (Phil 2:7) in order to be the Servant of the servants so that the servant should no longer be shamed to serve the Lord." "The wisdom of the Father sent down the light of the Godhead into the fragile vessel of our human nature." "Out of love for us he bound himself so tightly to us that his love took on our agony as its own, as if he could not wish to remain in heaven without us." "The Son came for the redemption of the human race, becoming Son of Man by reason of his human nature as he was Son of God by reason of his divine nature. Therefore, there are not two Sons, but only one Son."

Anthony can rightly be called the herald of the incarnate Son of God. For this reason, there is an intrinsic justification for the fact that, in later ages, he is depicted with the Infant Jesus on his arm. It is not necessary to reach back to any supposed apparition of the Christ Child. Anthony's Christology provides a sufficient basis.

Even the Shepherds of the Church Are in Need of Conversion

To Anthony it was clear that the alienation of so much of the religious movement of his time from the church could be attributed, to a great extent, to the official representatives of the church. Many clergy, neglecting their pastoral obligations, frequently scandalized the faithful by their way of life. To such clergy, Anthony spoke in clear and pointed language that challenged their conscience sharply. The points which he raised in this context may well have been, for the most part, the very matters expressed by the heretics in their criticism of the church. But his motivation was different. He did not wish his criticism to lead to a rejection of the church; but he did wish, with words that are open and almost shocking, to awaken reflection and conversion. He wished to help the church.

The clarity and sharpness with which Anthony spoke might astound us today. It is hardly possible for anyone today to call things by their true name so clearly without experiencing sanctions. Certainly, the abuses among the clergy which Anthony attacked are not present as extensively or as massively today as they were at that time.

But aside from that, it is noticeable that we today are very reserved about any internal criticism of the church. The mediaeval period, on the other hand, was well acquainted with such internal church criticism; concern about abuses was clearly expressed. From the time of the Reformation at the beginning of the sixteenth-century when new Christian communities arose to compete with the Catholic church, this sort of internal criticism moved to the background and could be expressed only with considerable caution. One did not want to provide propaganda material for these new communities by criticism of conditions within the church. That which could rightly have been seen earlier as a helpful criticism would now be seen as "dirtying one's own nest."

Anthony spoke clearly about the relation between the growth of heresy and the corruption of the clergy: "The priests of the church do not possess the light of wisdom, nor do they show true virtues in their actions. Hence the devil scatters the sheep and the thief, namely, the heretic, attracts them to himself."

He characterizes the way many pastors deal with their flocks in the following way: "Feed my sheep, says the Lord to Peter (Jn 21:17). Mark well. The Lord says three times: Feed my sheep. But not even once does he say: Shear them, or milk them."

He could become even more explicit: "At the time of Elias, the prophets of Baal called out and found no hearing. But in our days, they call and they are heard. They are placed in the highest positions so that they might fall even further. Once their voices were modest, their dress poor, their bodies emaciated, and their faces pale. But today, there is a glint in their eyes. Here they come in grand ornament and mitres. They stride behind their bellies; their faces are red; they are friends with sleep and enemies to prayer. Oh! let an Elias come. Yes, let an Elias come to strike down these priests of Baal and kill them."

Anthony held the mirror of self-knowledge before the members of religious orders as well. It may well be that experiences with the Augustinian canons at Coimbra have flowed into his words: "In the rule or statutes of their Order it is written that each monk or canon ought to have two or three shirts, and two pairs of shoes for summer and winter. When, at certain times and places and with nobody's fault, it happens that they do not have these things, they complain that the statutes of the order are not being fulfilled, and that terrible aberrations are involved. Behold, with what zeal they would follow the laws and prescriptions concerning the body. But the law of Jesus Christ they observe hardly at all, even though without this they cannot find salvation."

"The monks have falsified the rule of St. Benedict, and the canons have done the same with the rule of St. Augustine. In like manner, we could continue through the list of individual members of the orders who seek their own advantage and not the work of Jesus Christ (Phil 2:21)."

In this context, Anthony frequently addresses a problem which seems to be a perpetual temptation for life in the church: "What shall I say about the clergy and dignitaries in the church? When a bishop or prelate of the church fails against the regulations of Alexander or Innocent, or of any other pope, he will be cited immediately. After the citation will come the summons, after the summons will come the proof, and after the proof will come the removal from office. But if such a person has failed seriously against the Gospel of Christ, which we ought to follow above all other things, there is no one to cite him and no one to blame him, for all seek their own advantage rather than the work of Jesus Christ (Phil 2:31)."

The Style of Preaching in the Early Order of Friars Minor

In this first phase of Anthony's preaching activity in Italy from 1222-1224, something happens that is important not only for Anthony, but for the entire Order to which he belonged, and for the entire church. At the time of St. Anthony, the church made a clear distinction in styles of preaching. There was the so-called "exhortation," or the admonition and call to penance; and there was the thematic sermon in the proper sense. The exhortation, edifying in tone, in simple words summoned one to penance and to good works. For this, no particular theological education or homiletic training was necessary. Pope Innocent III had permitted this style of penitential preaching to St. Francis and his companions in the year 1209 when he gave his first approval to the primitive Rule of the Friars Minor.

The genuinely thematic sermon is described as "a presentation by means of divisions and distinctions." This presupposed systematic thinking as well as theological and homiletic education. This style of preaching was treasured highly. Even Francis, who was naturally more disposed to the exhortation — he filled its simplicity with his enlight-ened wisdom — tried to attempt a thematic sermon once. He had been invited by the pope to preach before himself and the cardinals. Cardinal Hugolino, a friend of the Saint, was concerned that Francis should make a good impres-sion and helped him to work out a thematic sermon which the Saint then learned by heart. Then, as he stood before the pope and the whole illustrious assembly of the papal court, he forgot the entire beautiful sermon. Instead, he gave an extemporaneous exhortation. But he spoke with such great spiritual fire that he actually spoke with his entire body. The pope and the cardinals were deeply moved.

In the early days of the Order in Umbria the simple exhortation may well have been sufficient since most of the people in that region were believers. Heresy and unbelief were not as widely spread as in other regions. But in upper Italy and France the situation was entirely differ-ent. There the faith was more severely threatened, and it was necessary to deal with heretics who were educated and ready for a fight. They were schooled in the art of argumen-tation and very familiar with the Bible. Anthony had shown himself to them as a mature person, and had had considerable success in effecting conversions. Not only did he offer a deeply theological basis for the church's faith in his sermons, but he was fully in command of the art of disputation and was far superior to the heretics in his knowledge of the Bible.

Francis Appoints Anthony as a Teacher of Theology for the Order

While Anthony was capable of this because of his education, most of his brothers in the Order lacked the most basic preparation. They could not meet the heretics in a way that would be useful in defending the church's doctrines. For a long time, Francis himself had been very reserved about the study of theology for his brothers. He was concerned that those who consciously called themselves "Lesser brothers" should not depart from the way of simplicity and humility.

But on the other hand, he saw himself and his Order to be called to the service of the church. And he recognized that his brothers could offer a very important service to the church if they brought a well-grounded theological knowledge into their sermons. Anthony could give such an education to his brothers. And, apparently, the brothers themselves had asked Anthony for this service. But he did not wish to do it without the approval of Francis. Thus, at the end of 1223 or the beginning of 1224, Francis wrote the following letter:

"To Brother Anthony, my bishop, I, Brother Francis, send greetings. It pleases me that you should teach sacred theology to the friars provided that through this study they do not extinguish the spirit of holy prayer and devotion, as is contained in the Rule."

The letter is brief. It is typical of Francis, and it is of great importance. After the death of Brother Peter Cathanii on March 10, 1221, Francis had designated Br. Elias of Cortona as his vicar, delegating to him all the power required for the leadership of the Order of Friars Minor. And as his behavior at the Pentecost chapter of 1221 indicated, Francis respected the decisions made by his vicar. But the decision involved in the letter to Anthony was of such significance for the Order that Francis, as the highest authority, would have to make it himself.

In view of the importance of the decision, the letter is extremely concise; but that is typical of Francis. It was indeed Francis who made the decision; but he said nothing more concerning the details of the structure, the development, the goals, or any other specifics that should be attended to in the study of theology. He felt himself to be incompetent in the matter and left it all in the hands of St.

Anthony. The very conciseness of the letter indicates what great trust Francis had in his brother, Anthony.

The letter of St. Francis contains no technical details but expresses an important spiritual direction. Francis does not reject the study of theology, although that has been claimed by many authors and is still maintained today. The letter clearly states the opposite. But it clearly expresses one point that occurs elsewhere in the writings of St. Francis: He rejects knowledge for its own sake, not wanting his brothers to fall into the temptation to acquire honor and respect before others through their knowledge.

In the view of St. Francis, the study of theology must be guided by a central concern: that the "spirit of holy prayer and devotion" — that is, the whole of one's relation with God — shall not be hindered or destroyed but shall be developed and deepened. In other words, knowledge in general, and theological knowledge specifically, is good and worth striving for when it leads a person to live his or her life honestly in the presence of God.

One could still think that the letter makes it clear that Francis approached the study of theology with considerable misgiving. For the letter contains the instruction that Anthony should take care that "in such studies the spirit of holy prayer and devotion" shall not be disturbed or extinguished. Yet it must be noted that in the Rule of the Order, Francis offers the same caution with respect to all forms of work, including manual labor. Anyone who wishes to claim that Francis was fundamentally opposed to the study of theology would have to maintain consistently that he was opposed to all forms of work for his brothers.

Yet Francis was well aware of the importance it had for his Order when he gave the "green light" for the study of theology in this brief letter to Anthony. But the exemplary life and the successful work of his brother, Anthony, made it easier for Francis to write the letter and to give this important task to Anthony.

"To Brother Anthony, my bishop." So reads the greeting in this letter. When Francis calls Anthony "his bishop," he certainly does not have in mind a position in the hierarchy of the church. Rather, he has in mind the office which he has given to Anthony. For the local church, the bishop is the custodian and administrator of the word of God. It is through him that Christ works and speaks. This is what Francis sees in the theologian as one who is learned about the things of God. He is a person who, as Francis says in his Testament, imparts "spirit and life." Such a person deserves honor and appropriate respect.

The Franciscan course of Studies in Bologna

Unfortunately, we do not know much about the activity of St. Anthony as a lector of theology for the friars. It is a quiet, ordinary task without much publicity. When things follow a steady course, there is not much attractive to recount. But so much is certain: that the course of studies of the Franciscans in Bologna goes back to Anthony. However, it cannot be proved with certainty that he was really the first lector of theology in the Order.

Bologna provided favorable conditions for a house of studies in the Order. The first university of Italy had been founded there in the year 1086. This university had a particularly good reputation because of the care given to the study of law. Anthony likely worked between 1223 and 1224 in the Franciscan convent of Santa Maria delle Pugiole. The Franciscan course of studies could profit much from that of the university: the use of books which the Franciscan Order could not acquire, and the cooperation of professors. In this phase, Anthony not only taught; he learned as well. The proximity of the university and the contact with the professors gave him the opportunity to continue the studies he had begun at Coimbra. Perhaps he was in Vercelli in 1224 to hear Thomas Gallus, the famous canon regular of St. Augustine. Thomas was abbot of the

Augustinian cloister near the basilica of St. Andrew in Vercelli. Because he came from the famous theological school of St. Victor at Paris, he had the surname "Gallus, the Gaul." He was the author of a great commentary on the mystical theology of Dionysius the Areopagite, a work that was of great importance in the Middle Ages. Anthony had good contacts with him. Here he was able to complete his education and to receive many valuable suggestions for other areas of his life. For Thomas Gallus was not only an important theologian; he was also very interested in and engaged in politics, though not always so successfully.

Thomas Gallus had a very high opinion of St. Anthony. Thus, he wrote: "Brother Anthony of the Franciscans, my good friend, strove to become acquainted with mystical theology. He was so successful in this that I can say of him what was said of John the Baptist: He was a bright light that shone outward through his good example."

IV.
ANTHONY IN
SOUTHERN FRANCE

The town of Vercelli, where Anthony made the acquaintance of Thomas Gallus, was already a good way along the journey from Bologna to France where Anthony was sent in the year 1224 after everything that had happened to him. It was probably his success in dealing with the Cathari in upper Italy that led to his being sent there. Although the Cathari had spread in upper Italy, their strongest territory was southern France. Their "capital city" in France was Albi. Hence, they were also known as Albigensians.

The Albigensians Become a Problem for the Church

The Albigensians were not satisfied simply with preaching their heretical doctrines. They aggressively attacked all representatives of ecclesiastical orthodoxy as well. Unfortunately, the latter often enough provided grounds for justified criticism. The Cathari struck a very sensitive nerve in the dignitaries of the church when they claimed that the members of the hierarchy ought to have no private possessions such as land-holdings; and that the hierarchy put pressure on the faithful to give a tenth of their goods to the church. In this respect, the Cathari were of interest also to the secular authorities, who provided support for the

heretics. They did this not out of sympathy for the doctrines of the Cathari, but with the hope that they would
profit from these controversies about church property.

The alarm of the popes can be seen in a letter which
Pope Honorius III sent to the French King Louis in 1223: "It
will certainly disturb you to see that, in one of the most
promising regions of your kingdom, the region of Albi,
heretics fight openly and boldly against the church. They
wish to erode the Christian life and to tear apart Jesus
Christ . . . The efforts that have been made up till now to
uproot this heresy have been almost useless, since the
heresy is spreading again."

How Is One to Deal with the Albigensians?

Efforts had been made for some time to stem the tide
of the heresy or even to extinguish it. The first person
involved in this work was St. Dominic, who died in 1221.
He went about his work for the church vigorously not only
with his sermons, but also with his exemplary life of
poverty and sanctity in Languedoc. His brothers, following him in this, also had success. But impressive mass-con-
versions were not to be expected in dealing with such a
large number of fanatic heretics who were unwavering
under persecution, even to the joyful acceptance of death.

Unfortunately, other kinds of approaches were tried
which involved the use of force against the Albigensians,
and which even took the form of a crusade. The southern
French Cathari were far more dangerous to the church
because of their closed dogmatic positions, their good
organization, and their political power. The trigger for the
bloody wars against the Albigensians came in 1208. The
papal legate, Peter of Castelnau, was murdered. He had
gone to see Count Raymond of Toulouse to demand the
return of property that had been taken from the church.

Pope Innocent III praised the attempts to convert the

heretics through preaching. But even this man, the most powerful of all popes, found that his patience was coming to an end. Certainly, the church had encouraging words of praise for the missionary preachers of the faith. But for the decisive success, Rome now looked not so much to conversion as to extermination. Pope Innocent III excommunicated the Count of Toulouse. That can be seen as an appropriate reaction on the part of the church; but Innocent III went further, declaring war on the Albigensians by proclaiming a crusade against them. Even the physical destruction of these heretics was praised as a work pleasing to God.

One would have reckoned with a short war or crusade. But the frightful affair lasted over twenty years. The Albigensian war, under the official leadership of the abbot-legate Arnaldus Amalrici, developed into a power-struggle between the French army under Simon de Montfort on the one side and Count Raymond VI and Peter of Aragon on the other. It turned out to be a bloody affair among the nobility. Not even the victory of Simon de Montfort, which was won at a terrible cost, assured success. This came only with the intervention of the central French power in the person of King Louis VIII, who brought about the Peace of Meaux in 1229.

But even with this, the Cathari were not totally eliminated. It was only in 1330, thanks to the Inquisition, that the Albigensians were fully overcome. The French King was the only one who really gained any profit from these harsh, unchristian wars, since the lands of the Count of Toulouse and others of the nobility, who either were heretics or declared themselves to be heretics, went to the French crown.

The Relation of St. Francis to France

This was the situation into which Anthony was sent in 1224–1225 with his missionary mandate to France. The

founder of his Order had a special concern for France. His
mother had come from there; his father had profitted
greatly from his business in the French market. He himself
had sung the songs of the French "troubadours" in his
youth, even though he did not know the French language
well. He himself wished to choose France as his field of
activity; but his friend, Cardinal Hugolino, was able to
convince him that it was urgent for him to remain in Italy
so that he could personally clarify the many problematic
issues that were arising. Then Francis sent Brother Pacific,
the "King of Verses," to France together with other brothers. While these brothers succeeded in winning some men
for the Order, they do not seem to have developed any
particular fame for controversy with the heretics. Because
of the nature of the church's problems, the Franciscans
needed to be engaged in southern France in a different and
more successful way. Anthony was chosen for this task.
Naturally this did not happen without the knowledge and
agreement of St. Francis.

Francis Confirms His Brother Anthony in His Task

In his own way, Francis gave his confirmation for the
mission of St. Anthony to southern France. Anthony
probably arrived in Arles around the end of the month of
September 1224. Brother John Bonelli, the provincial
minister of the Provence, had called his brothers to a provincial chapter on September 29, the feast of St. Michael
the Archangel, to discuss "things that refer to God," as the
Rule puts it. Anthony participated in this provincial chapter of the brothers. And since his fame as a great preacher
had preceded him, he was given the task of addressing the
brothers gathered there in chapter.

What happened on that occasion is narrated by Brother

Thomas of Celano in his first Legenda of Francis, written in 1228–1229 and, therefore, during the life-time of Anthony. "I will give one example from among many which I know from witnesses. Brother John of Florence had been appointed by St. Francis as minister in the Provence. When he was celebrating a chapter in the same province, the Lord God, in his customary mercy, opened the door of speech to him and made all the brothers well-disposed and attentive listeners. Among the brothers was one who was a priest of great renown but of even more noteworthy life, Monaldo by name. His virtue was grounded in humility, supported by frequent prayer, and preserved by the shield of patience. Brother Anthony was also present at the chapter. The Lord had opened his mind to understand the Scriptures and to speak before the entire assembly about Jesus in words that were sweeter than syrup or honey from the comb.

"While he was preaching with great fervor and devotion to the brothers on this topic, 'Jesus of Nazareth, King of the Jews' (Jn 19:19), Brother Monaldo looked toward the door of the house where the brothers had gathered. There, with his bodily eyes, he saw St. Francis raised in the air with his hands extended as though on a cross, and blessing his brothers. And all were seen to be filled with the consolation of the Holy Spirit. And the great joy they experienced made them quite ready to believe what was told to them concerning the presence and appearance of their glorious father." This occurrence was seen as very important in the Middle Ages. It was frequently expressed in artistic form, as, for example, in the fresco-cycle of the life of St. Francis by Giotto in the upper church of St. Francis in Assisi. It must have been seen as a strong authentification of Anthony given by Francis himself. Furthermore, Francis had received the imprints of the wounds of the crucified Jesus around the same time, that is, on September 14, 1224. And Anthony's sermon at Arles had been about the inscription on the cross.

Work in Montpellier

From Arles, Anthony journeyed to Montpellier. During the wars with the Cathari mentioned above, this was the military center for the orthodox. An educational center whose purpose was to prepare people for missionary work among the Cathari was located there as well.

It had become ever more clear to responsible people that the confrontation with the heretics required, above all, theologians who were equal to the Cathari in their formal schooling, but especially in their knowledge of the Holy Scriptures. Already in 1217, Pope Honorius III had turned with this concern to the professors at the University of Paris: "With this, our apostolic letter, we ask your university and appeal to it to send some of your members to us for the purpose of defending the cause of Christ and of devoting themselves zealously to instruction, preaching, and exhortation."

Anthony was prepared to offer to the church the sort of service for which the pope had appealed to the theologians. He had been sent to southern France for this purpose. He could bring with him the experience he had gained in a similar mission in northern Italy. Like the Dominicans, and on good terms with them, he went about the task of educating brothers and priests in an appropriate manner. He was concerned also with developing a knowledge of the faith among the faithful and with cultivating a life consonant with the faith so that the faithful might be made immune to the teachings of the Cathari. In this area, there was much that had to be restored to the church.

In Toulouse, the Stronghold of the Cathari

Anthony was not the sort to avoid unpleasant confrontations and to remain, so to say, on the periphery where the missionary would not have to experience the full impact of the problems. In upper Italy he had gone to

Rimini which was the center of spiritual power for the Cathari. He followed precisely the same procedure in southern France. Intrepidly he went to Toulouse, the stronghold of the Cathari, where he preached the faith of the church in his convincing style and engaged in public discussions with the heretics who, naturally, sent their most experienced people for this purpose.

From every angle, the Saint was in a position to disarm and convince his opponents. Since his simple habit revealed even externally his authentic poverty, it was impossible to maintain that he did not live according to the teaching of Christ, as could be said of many of the dignitaries of the church. And this poor friar revealed such an extensive knowledge of the Holy Scriptures in the debates that no one could challenge his argumentation.

He was called the "Hammer of Heretics." But he never took up the hammer of external force against the heretics. It was his arguments, coming as they did from an outstanding intellect, that destroyed the arguments of his opponents like a spiritual hammer.

It is noteworthy that in his sermons, Anthony speaks directly of the errors of the Cathari only rarely. He was apparently of the opinion that the point of preaching was to strengthen the faith by giving a convincing and positive presentation of the Christian faith and of the life that flowed from this faith. In this way, the return of the heretics and their followers to the church could be facilitated. The proper place for the direct, critical confrontation with the heretics was in the discussions. Unfortunately, no detailed reports of these discussions have been preserved.

Guardian at Puy-en-Velay

The Saint did not remain long at Toulouse. He had made a break-through there; but he did not want to rest in his victories, so to say. The beginning that had been made and the way that had been opened he could turn over to the brothers whom he had trained for the work. Naturally, they could benefit from the prestige that their Brother Anthony had won, even if they themselves never reached the same stature.

Anthony moved to a new field of endeavor which had been assigned to him. He became guardian of the convent of his Order at Puy-en-Velay. As a term used to designate the leader of the local community among the Friars Minor, the word "guardian" means literally "watcher" or "one who attends to the well-being of others." The place to which Anthony was assigned, about three-hundred kilometers northeast of Toulouse, was considered to be the "Holy City" of France; for it was there that a famous, miraculous image of the "Black Mother of God" was venerated. There were practically no heretics in this center of the ancient, traditional life of faith. The people were faithful to the church's teaching. Indeed, in the sanctuary of the Mother of God they had a spiritual center of practical faith.

Here it was only a question of supporting and strengthening the faith that was already present. It was a field for the pastoral care of individuals. To this Anthony devoted himself with zeal and love. A later account of Saint Anthony's work at Puy-en-Velay states: "He led the brothers with great circumspection and goodness, and led the people to a Christian life through his tireless preaching and his heroic example."

At the Synod in Bourges

November 30, 1225, is a prominent date in the life of St. Anthony. Simon de Sully, the archbishop of Bourges, convoked a national synod on that day. Bourges was the capital city of the duchy of Berry and the primatial See of Aquitaine.

The synod, regarded as one of very great significance, was convoked to consult on the situation of the church in France, to take measures to clean up the situation in southern France, and to align it with the Catholic church. Pope Honorius III had sent a legate to take part in it. There were six archbishops, about a hundred bishops, prelates, and religious superiors. Also political figures appeared, such as Amanry of Montfort and Raymond of Toulouse.

Many of those who showed up at the synod wanted to see the heretical teachings of the Cathari contained, and if possible, exterminated. But they were just as interested in extending their own power. This they could do "with the blessing of the church" if someone who fought them over territorial issues either was a heretic or was suspected of heresy. As the heretic in that age was considered to be as free as a bird, so his property was free game for those who were more powerful. From this perspective, even the archbishop of Bourges wore two hats. On the one hand, as the metropolitan, he had the ecclesiastical obligation to control heresy; on the other hand, he was in charge of a very wealthy and influential household which was naturally very concerned about its property.

Anthony's invitation to this synod, says something about the fame which he had acquired. But would Archbishop Simon de Sully have invited him if he had known in advance what was to take place? For Anthony clearly recognized the sore points among the representatives of the ecclesiastical hierarchy and the disastrous effects of all this on the people. Not mincing his words, he took as his own the word of the Apostle Paul to his disciple, Timothy: "Preach the word, be urgent in season and out of season, convince, rebuke, and exhort, be unfailing in patience and in teaching" (2 Tim 4:2). Anthony did not succumb to the temptation that is so common at such gatherings, namely, to speak only about those who were not present, that is, to denounce the heretics and their errors and evil ways.

Those who were gathered for the synod could do nothing to change the heretics. But they could change themselves. And in this way, they could remove the stumbling block and take the wind out of the sails of the heretics. This was exactly what Anthony preached with blunt clarity. The gathering was subjected to a severe sermon full of clear and serious charges. Anthony did not think he had to be particularly reserved in the presence of his host, nor did he feel that courtesy should keep him from pointing out the weaknesses of his host. "Now I have a word to address to you who wear the mitre." So, even the archbishop Simon de Sully would have his faults held before his eyes.

Apparently Anthony did not first ask himself whether he was held in sufficiently high esteem to make such accusations in the circle of people gathered there. He feared no sanctions. And there were none. Was his reputation already so great that none of those who were called to account dared to take action against him? But with the archbishop he was successful. He had awakened the sleeping conscience of this prince of the church. Simon de Sully, shocked at what he saw when Anthony held the mirror before him, underwent a total conversion and in tears asked Anthony to hear his confession and to pray for him.

Custos in Limoges

Naturally the members of the Order held their confrere in high regard and had great trust in him, all of which became apparent when the Order designated Anthony as custos with his residence in Limoges. At that time, the great provinces of the Order were divided into smaller jurisdictional territories with a number of convents. These territories were called custodies, under the leadership of a custos.

Anthony worked as custos of Limoges from 1226 until Pentecost of 1227. Among the concerns of his office was particularly the care for the spiritual development of the brethren. The Rule of the Order at that time described the tasks of the superiors in the following way: "They shall look after the brothers and admonish them, and correct them in humility and love, without commanding anything that is against their soul — their conscience — and our Rule."

Since at that period of the Order's history the lay brothers were often in the majority and there were many convents that had no priest, it was often a very important job for a custos to travel from house to house to give the brothers the opportunity to receive the sacrament of penance. We know this concretely about Br. Jordan of Giano who, as custos of Thuringia, was the only priest in the custody. He saw to it that another of the brothers was ordained to the priesthood so that he himself would not have to be forever on the road in order to provide the opportunity of confession for the brothers.

In this phase when the Order entrusted Anthony with affairs internal to the community, the Saint withdrew from the front lines of the battle against the heretics; for there were hardly any heretics in the area of Limoges. So it was possible for Anthony to devote himself entirely to internal affairs of the Order. Among these concerns was the theological education of the brethren and some training in how to debate with the heretics. Beside this, he was able to give himself to the task of strengthening the faith of people whose hold on the faith was often a mere formality. He devoted himself to that area of work that can be called the "inner mission."

As custos, Anthony found it necessary to be constantly on the road in order to seek out the brothers in the various settlements. On these trips, when he passed through villages and towns, he used the opportunity to strengthen the people in faith and to point out to them the ways of

God. People of that age were used to having wandering preachers come and preach a message which, often enough, was not the authentic gospel message of Christ. He was particularly concerned for those who had fallen into sin and had become victims of evil. As his sermon outlines indicate, he always reminded sinners of God's loving mercy, and reminded them that God's mercy is greater than any malicious failure on the part of a sinful human being.

In this way, even during this period of his life, Anthony carried on a very lively preaching activity, but few details of it remain for us. Of this period it is claimed that the churches were frequently incapable of holding all the people who wanted to hear him. In such instances, Anthony preached outdoors. We know specifically that he preached at the cemetery of St. Paul in Limoges on All Souls Day in 1226, and that he preached once in an open field in the village of Saint Junien near Limoges.

Again a Withdrawal into Solitude

As custos of Limoges, Anthony established a new friary in Brive, 100 kilometers south of Limoges. This had been a favorite stopping place for him where he had chosen a grotto as his hermit's cell. He liked to withdraw to this place in order to break up the periods of strenuous activity with regular periods of contemplative quiet. This was exactly the way Francis had lived. As much as he felt compelled to preach the good news of the Kingdom of God to the people, still he withdrew to solitude over and over again for shorter or longer periods of undisturbed recollection with God.

Anthony had experienced and wished to experience again and again what he himself had described in the following words: "The Lord appears to those who with-draw from the busy world into solitude and rest." He understood the importance of the rhythm of contempla-tion and activity, particularly for someone who is to proclaim the Kingdom of God. Christ himself showed this rhythm to his twelve apostles. For Scripture says: "And he appointed twelve, to be with him, and to be sent out to preach" (Mk 3:14). To be with him, the Lord, and to be sent out by him. This was crucial for the entire life of Anthony. As much as he was engaged in the activity of the aposto-late, he never gave himself exhaustively to his work, but was always able to draw back from it. Brother John Rigaldus, who wrote his account between 1293 and 1317, remarked about Anthony's work in southern France: "The educated people were amazed at the sharpness of his mind and at his eloquence . . . He understood how to direct his speech to the particular audience so that those who were in error left their false ways, sinners were brought to conversion and repentance, and the good felt themselves called to do still better. In general, no one went home unsatisfied."

Anthony's stay at Brive has remained a living tradi-tion. It is associated with many wonderful events which the tradition locates there. The most famous is the miracle of bilocation: Anthony was seen at two different places. He stood in Montpellier preaching in the pulpit in a church that was filled to overflowing. There he remembered sud-denly that his confreres at home were waiting for him to pray the divine Office. He resolved this conflict of obliga-tions by becoming present at both places. Theologians trained in parapsychology assume that bilocation is pos-sible and claim that in one place there is a physical presence, and in the other a psychic presence; a phenome-non that can be explained only with great difficulty. Whatever the case may be, these accounts show that one did not hesitate to attribute apparently impossible things to Anthony.

The Death of Saint Francis

St. Francis died on the evening of October 3, 1226, in a small hut near the church of the Portiuncula which is situated on the plain below Assisi. Although he had remained the highest authority (minister general) of his Order until his death, already at the Pentecost chapter of the Order in 1220, he had appointed Peter Cathanii as vicar general and delegated to him all the powers necessary for taking care of the business of the Order. After the death of Peter Cathanii on March 10, 1221, Francis appointed Brother Elias of Cortona as vicar general. We spoke of this earlier; but we will repeat the matter briefly here, since it is of particular importance for the final years of St. Francis' life.

It was a blessing that Francis had appointed vicars for the conduct of the more technical, jurisdictional matters involved in the leadership of the Order, and had given them the corresponding power. When Francis took this step in 1220, he most likely did it with the awareness that administrative and juridical matters were not his strength, but the Order could not be led well without looking after such matters. His charism, therefore, sought brothers who were capable of mastering the institutional dimension. Toward the end of his life, he was no longer physically capable of administering the Order. It was not only the matter of his frequent illness and his failing sight that made it necessary for him to have care. Since the stigmatisation in the middle of September, 1224, he lived the last two years of his life quite literally as one who had been crucified, even with nails in the wounds of his hands and feet. It was a good fortune for the Order that the administrative leadership of the Order could be taken over by Br. Elias as vicar general.

It was Br. Elias, therefore, who informed the Order of the death of St. Francis in his letter of October 4, 1226, to Br. Gregory of Naples, the provincial of France. In the same letter, Elias made it known that the saint had carried the wounds of Christ in his body.

The General Chapter of Pentecost, 1227

The Rule of the Franciscan Order that has been in effect since 1223 has the following to say concerning the office of the general: "All the brothers are bound always to have one of the brothers of this Order as the minister general and servant of the entire fraternity, and they are bound strictly to obey him. At his death, the ministers provincial and the custodes are to elect a successor at the Pentecost chapter at which the ministers provincial are always bound to convene in the place designated by the minister general; and they shall do this once every three years or at a longer or shorter interval as decided by the aforementioned minister." In accordance with this prescription, Br. Elias called the general chapter of Pentecost, 1227, at Assisi. According to the Rule, Anthony was obliged to come to this general chapter by virtue of his position as custos. On May 29, 1227, Br. John Parenti was elected as minister general of the Order. He had been born in Civitacastellana, and had been a judge before his entrance into the Order. Prior to his election as general of the Order, he had been provincial in Spain.

V.
ANTHONY BECOMES PROVINCIAL OF THE ROMAGNA

At the general chapters of the Franciscans, the offices of leadership were open and could be filled with new appointments. The changes that took place at the general chapter of 1227 involved Anthony. He was appointed provincial of the northern Italian province of the Romagna. Unlike Francis, the new general, John Parenti, did not have a vicar general to take over the organizational tasks of the Order. Thus, the decision to name Anthony as provincial of the Romagna was essentially the decision of John Parenti himself. It is said that, after the office of the minister general, this would have been perhaps the most difficult and the most important position in the Order.

The Situation of the Province of the Romagna

Six years earlier, Anthony would have been overlooked in the distribution of the brothers among the provinces had not Br. Gratian, provincial of the Romagna, had sympathy and taken him to his province. With respect to its extent, the number of its friaries, and the number of brothers, the Romagna was one of the largest provinces of the Order. It was later recognized that the territory of the province was too large for uniform administration and guidance. Hence, the provinces of Genoa, Milan, Bologna, and Venice were created out of the territory of this single province.

Anthony was familiar with the territory and the many levels of problems in the province from the time of his preaching activity in the years 1222-1224. Even though the battle against the erroneous teachings of the Cathari and the Waldensians had never escalated in northern Italy to the extent that the wars against the Albigensians had in southern France, still there were many adherents to these anti-ecclesiastical groups. Anthony saw it as an important task for himself and his brothers to work against these movements. Precisely in northern Italy the cities had become very strong and self-conscious. They had begun to develop an urban, middle-class culture which was not well formed in the faith of the church. The developed self-consciousness of the urban communes frequently came into conflict with the episcopal sovereigns. The widespread development of the monetary system led to sharp distinctions between the rich and the poor. Usury was common-place and caused much misery. The constant political conflicts among groups struggling for power were an on-going and dangerous problem.

Anthony was not ignorant of the many levels of problems that awaited him. But his primary concern was the care of the brothers of the Order. He would have to reckon with the need of visiting the many friaries in order to become acquainted with the brothers, to give them the opportunity to express their concerns and problems, to instruct them in living consistently in the manner of the Gospel, and in general, to help them to be faithful to their work for the Kingdom of God in accordance with their vocation.

The Development of Convents Within the Order

Since Anthony traveled so widely both as a wandering preacher and now as a minister provincial, we must ask exactly how these journeys were carried out. In the early period, the brothers of St. Francis had hardly any established settlements of the Order to depend on in their apostolic journeys. They would spend the night wherever the opportunity presented itself; with generous people, in cellars, in archways, and with preference, in churches. Looking back on the adventurous early period of his fraternity, Francis himself speaks of this in his Testament: "And we were glad to stay in churches."

But even Francis recognized that his fraternity needed more stable structures, and that more permanent friaries would be necessary so that the brothers would know to what small community they belonged, and who, as guardian, was responsible for them and their needs. It was not a reluctant Yes that Francis gave to the founding of stable convents. Already very early in the beginning of the Order he himself had established a genuine convent for seven brothers on Monte Luco above Spoleto. (There is also a grotto of St. Anthony on Monte Luco, which would indicate that the Saint had visited the place.) In his Testament, Francis gives his full approval to the development in the Order leading to permanent convents: "The brothers should take care not to accept churches, poor dwellings, or anything that is built for them, unless they are in harmony with the poverty which we have promised in the Rule." Thus, Francis was of the opinion that even in the changed circumstances that brought about more stable living conditions, his brothers were able to observe the ideal of poverty. He was intelligent, and therefore did not leave the Order bound rigidly to the forms of the beginning without compromise. He was capable of adapting to the necessary developments without giving up his ideals.

As a result of this development which was approved by Francis, the Franciscan Order especially in Italy built a rather dense network of convents and hermitages which frequently were just a day's journey apart. Hence on his visitation-trips throughout the province entrusted to his care, Anthony could count on staying for the most part in houses of the Order.

Even Saints Fail

After his appointment as provincial of the Romagna, Anthony left Assisi for an area of the province that was not familiar to him from the time of his earlier preaching activity in 1222-1224; namely, the border area near Trieste. It is possible that he traveled to Trieste by ship from Ravenna, a city known to him earlier. From there he was able to travel throughout all of Istria, winning many men to the Order, and founding a number of convents, including those at Trieste, Pula, Muggia, and a place that today is known as Porec. But in Friaul things did not work out so well. Things went well for Anthony in Cividale, Gemona, and Görz. But in Udine he experienced a failure which was not even twisted into a success by later legend. Those who had invited him to preach at Udine were apparently a hopeless minority who had totally miscalculated the realities of the situation. At any event, the following happened. Anthony went to a section of Udine called Pracchiuso, and climbed a tree so as to preach better from an elevated position. For reasons unknown to us, it seemed impossible to preach in the church. But when Anthony had taken his place in the tree, a group of local fanatics shouted the most evil insults at him. He gave up his attempt and climbed down from the tree.

The situation in Pracchiuso must have been quite unusual. Otherwise, Anthony would not have given up so quickly. Remarkably, the legend does not attempt to turn this failure into a success as happened with the sermon to the fish in Rimini. Was Udine perhaps so remote for the later authors of the Legenda that they felt no inclination to depict the miraculous, transformative power of the Saint?

Leave the Saints in Peace

In the case of Gemona, the interest of the writer of the Legenda was alert to show how consistent and unyielding Anthony could be. When Anthony arrived at Gemona, the people were in the process of building a chapel. But the work had come to a standstill because they had no means of transporting the necessary building materials to the spot. Now, a farmer with a cart passed by. Anthony asked him to put himself at the service of the good cause. But the farmer did not wish to help. He lied to the Saint, telling him that he could not put his cart at the disposal of the builders because it contained the corpse of his son. The son, however, had merely fallen asleep. After he had gone on a short way, the father wished to awaken his son to tell him how he had deceived Anthony. To his horror, he discovered that his son was really dead. He turned around immediately and begged Anthony for forgiveness. The son returned to life on the spot. In his biography of Anthony, P. Scandaletti uses an Italian proverb to comment: "Scherza coi fanti, ma lascia stare i santi" (Play jokes with children, but leave the saints in peace.)

What should we think about this story? Does it not depict a man whom one dared not approach too closely without risking the danger of death? And this man was a saint! We certainly do not think of Anthony in such terms.

But if we abstract from the question as to whether this actually happened or not and search for the deeper meaning of the story, it appears that we have before us a perfect example of what the philosophy of religion calls the phenomenon of the "sacred."

When a person encounters the sacred, he or she feels deeply touched at the core of human existence. The feelings associated with such an encounter manifest a distinctive tension. They oscillate between a fear that wishes to maintain distance and a fascination that wants to draw closer. On the one hand, the encounter with the holy can engender the sense of a beatifying, blessed mystery. On the other hand, the holy can create the feeling that the human person has encountered an unapproachable sovereignty, indeed, a dangerous and superior mystery. Certainly, the author of this account did not approach his work from the perspective of the philosophy of religion. But he exactly reflects the elements that are proper to the encounter with the holy. The farmer in the story experiences both: the threatening, and the beatifying. These primal human experiences are given concrete form in this story. One ought not try to deceive holy people. If one attempts to do so nonetheless, one will be punished.

The Dilemma of Letters of Safe-Conduct and Privileges

Anthony traveled far in the region of Venice and then in Lombardy. A number of cities claim that the Saint stayed within their walls: Conegliano, Treviso, Venice, Trent, Riva on Lago di Garda, Verona, and Bassano di Grappa. In the last-named town, the brothers had encountered problems which, at that time, had been experienced in many places. There was a small church there, dedicated to St. Donatus, which was cared for by the brothers in an adjoining convent. The church and convent had become a political issue because Pope Gregory IX had taken a stand in their favor. In a letter of October 20, 1227, he placed the church and convent under papal protection. In a document of October 21, 1227, it was made clear that the church and convent were withdrawn from the jurisdiction of the patriarch of Aquileia and the bishop of Padua. The pope made both of these church authorities responsible for the protection of the friars.

The reason for this intervention on the part of the highest ecclesisatical authority were: The church of St.

Donatus and all the property belonging to it were to be given over to the friars by the bishop of Vicenza. Naturally the bishop was anything but enthused about this. But the pope was particularly concerned with the good of the friars. As Cardinal Hugolino, he had been a faithful friend and helper of St. Francis. He was very concerned to support the friars in their work and to secure them against all obstacles. The houses of the friars stood for the preservation and strengthening of the true faith. Under papal protection, the church and convent of the brothers became an untouchable place of asylum to which one could flee in times of war and where a person could find protection from the chicanery of the authorities.

In this situation, Anthony had to come to Bassano di Grappa by virtue of his position as the responsible provincial. Here was the beginning of a development which would bring many difficulties to the Order. Certainly, the Order could feel pleased that the pope extended such protection to it because this meant that the pope saw the friars as a truly dependable cadre which he could call on at any time in the pursuit of ecclesiastical-political goals. But in the long run, the proliferation of privileges for the Order led to numerous conflicts and controversies with bishops and with the parish clergy.

St. Francis seems to have been intuitively aware of the problems which would arise here when he wrote in his Testament shortly before his death: "In virtue of obedience, I firmly command all my brothers, wherever they may be, not to petition the Roman curia, either personally or through an intermediary, for a papal brief, whether it concerns a church or any other place, or even in order to preach, or because they are being persecuted. If they are not welcome somewhere, they should flee to another country where they can do penance with God's blessing."

As we can see today, the case of Bassano di Grappa gave rise to a dilemma for the Order. On the one side, there was the prohibition against asking for papal briefs and privileges on the part of the Order's founder. Nothing was said about privileges granted by the pope unsolicited. On the other side, there was the attempt of the pope to assure the activity of the Order through letters and privileges. We would certainly like to know what position Anthony took in this dilemma. Had he recognized the growing problem? Unfortunately, the sources for his life give us no assistance here. Apparently the authors of the Legenda were not interested in such questions. They paid more attention to miracles. And, with respect to the remainder of his life, these sources narrate many miracles.

Restless Wandering

His visitation trips to the houses of the friars brought Anthony to extensive travels in Lombardy also. Thus, he came to Milan, Como, Bienno in val Camonica, Cremona, Brescia, Bergamo, Varese, and Mantua. Finally, he arrived at Padua, where he had his permanent residence from 1228. At first, he remained there only a few months. At this time he began the task of writing his sermon materials, a series of sermon-outlines intended for the use and the education of his confreres.

As provincial, he could not remain permanently at one and the same place and simply summon his brothers to himself. He had to go out to visit them. Hence, he came to Ferrara. In connection with this visit, a remarkable miracle is narrated which Anthony worked on behalf of an innocent person who was suspected of a crime.

A certain knight suspected his wife of adultery. She had given birth to a child whose skin was of a remarkably dark color. For the knight, this was "the proof" that she had had relations with a black man. No assurances of her innocence on the part of the woman could calm the knight's anger. He simply did not believe her. Their social circle in Ferrara had a wonderful topic for gossip. When Anthony arrived at the city, he was told that this apparently innocent woman was struggling to preserve her good name. This must have happened on the day when the gossip had reached a high-point because of fact that the infant was about to be baptized. Anthony intervened to clarify the situation. He instructed the infant to reveal the name of its father. The infant pointed to the knight and said loudly and with unmistakable clarity: "It is he." The mother's innocence was publicly confirmed.

The many places that retain a living memory of a visit by St. Anthony are not limited to the former territory of the Romagna province. A remarkable number of places out-side the provincial territory also have such traditions, for example, in Tuscany, and Umbria, etc. Here we will name only: Monte Luco near Spoleto, Buonriposo near Fossato, Speco di San Urbano, Montecasale, Cerbaiolo near Arezzo.

How did it come about that he visited these houses of other provinces? It could be that on the occasion of work trips to Rome or Assisi, Anthony interrupted his journey for a period of rest. Could it also be surmised that Anthony sought opportunities for complete isolation and for that contemplation which was so dear to him by staying in houses of other provinces, even if only for a short time, since there he would surely be unreachable by the pressure of the brothers of his own province? Even Francis had often taken refuge in solitary places where he could not be reached — as, for example, when he observed a forty-day fast alone on an island in Lake Trasimene.

In Rome and Assisi

It is estimated that Anthony was seldom really in Rome and Assisi. When "Rome" is taken to be equivalent to "papal curia," then we must recall that, at the time of Anthony, the papal curia was not always present in Rome, but resided in various Italian cities.

The first verifiable meeting of the Saint with the papal court in Rome took place at Easter of 1228. Anthony was in Rome because of affairs of the Order. Even then there were questions about how certain statements in the Rule of the Order were to be understood and explained. Certainly, we know hardly anything about the discussions or the results of the discussions concerning the particular questions. But the fact that Anthony was entrusted to take part in these discussions indicates clearly the degree of trust that the Order placed in him. The early Legenda do not seem to be interested at all in the details of these affairs. They were concerned especially with wonderful events that contributed to the fame of their hero. And, for this purpose, there were marvelous things to tell concerning this visit in Rome.

Pope Gregory IX (1227-1241), who knew the Order of St. Francis well, and many cardinals who were with him wished to hear Anthony preach. The impact of the Saint must have been exceptionally great, for the pope described him publicly as the "Repository of Holy Scripture."

The "Fioretti," a late collection of wonderful stories about Francis and his brothers, narrates the following concerning the sermon of Anthony at Rome: Anthony "preached once during a consistory of the pope and cardinals. Men of many nations had gathered for this consistory: Greeks, Latins, French, Germans, Slavs, English, and representatives of other peoples of the earth. Inflamed by the Holy Spirit, he preached and explained the word of God so effectively, devoutly, subtly, clearly, and understandably that all who were assembled at that consistory, although they spoke different languages, clearly and distinctly heard and understood every one of his words as if he had spoke in each of their languages. They were all astounded, for it seemed to them that the ancient miracle of Pentecost had been renewed, when by the power of the Holy Spirit the Apostles spoke in different languages. And in amazement, they said to one another:

"Is he not a Spaniard? How then are we all hearing him in the language of the country where we were born?" The pope also took to heart the profound content of the sermon and was so moved with wonder that he said: "Truly this is the Ark of the Covenant and the Repository of Holy Scripture."

This account shows how a later tradition honored the great preacher of the word of God and attempted to explain the exceptional effectiveness of his preaching.

Anthony himself had the following to say concerning the Pentecostal gift of tongues: "He speaks in foreign tongues who is filled with the Holy Spirit. These foreign tongues are the testimony that we give for Christ, namely, humility, poverty, patience, and obedience. When others see these virtues in us, we speak to them. Our speech is powerful when our works speak. I implore you, therefore, let your mouths be silent and your works speak. Our life is so full of beautiful words and so empty of good works."

With these words, Anthony refuses to limit the work of the Holy Spirit to the exceptional and the unique and extends it to the realm of every-day experience. The Holy Spirit unites himself with the disciple of Christ in such a way that, from outside, it is impossible to discern how far the work of the Spirit reaches and how far the work of human beings.

Anthony speaks of the silent miracles which make it possible for human beings to give genuine testimony to Christ. This witness, however, consists not only in the unity of the Word, but also in the multiplicity of works. Indeed, the multiple language of our works has greater convincing power as testimony because the human person is committed to the truth with his or her life. It is in this way that Anthony envisions the fulfillment of the saying of Jesus: "But you shall receive power when the Holy Spirit has come upon you; and you shall be my witnesses in Jerusalem and in all Judea and Samaria and to the end of the earth" (Acts 1:8).

Anthony certainly did not return to his province from Rome without having informed the minister general, Br. John Parenti, about what he had accomplished and what he was unable to accomplish in Rome because of the pope's departure from Rome shortly after the feast of Easter.

Francis is Canonized

It is highly probable that Anthony was in Assisi on July 16, 1228, when Francis was canonized. Since Anthony was the minister provincial of one of the Italian provinces, it would have been unusual had he not participated in this great event. Thus, he would have experienced the magnificence of the occasion as it is described in the first Legenda of Francis written by Thomas of Celano.

It was a momentous occasion when Pope Gregory IX spoke the following words: "To the praise and glory of Almighty God, the Father, Son, and Holy Spirit, and of the glorious Virgin Mary and of the blessed Apostles Peter and Paul, and to the honor of the glorious Roman Church, and after hearing the advice of our brothers and of the other prelates, we decree that the most blessed father Francis, whom the Lord has glorified in heaven and whom we venerate on earth, shall be enrolled in the catalogue of saints and that his feast shall be celebrated on the day of his death."

On the very day of the canonization, Pope Gregory IX laid the cornerstone for the construction of the church which was to be built in honor of St. Francis and was to serve as his burial place.

Scandal About the Transfer of the Remains of St. Francis

The construction of the church of St. Francis proceeded with energy. Thanks to the oversight and energetic leadership of Br. Elias, the work had progressed far enough by May 25, 1230, that it was possible to dedicate the church and transfer the remains of St. Francis to this, his burial place. For this reason, the minister general, Br. John Parenti, had convoked a general chapter of the Order at Assisi. As a provincial, Anthony was obliged to come to the general chapter. So he experienced how the transfer of the remains of St. Francis, which was planned to be a joyous celebration, was turned into a confusing fiasco.

As the solemn procession arrived at the new church, the militia of the city stepped in to close and barricade the doors. They permitted no one but Br. Elias and a few dependable people to enter the church. Naturally, those who had been kept out by trickery and force rebelled against such treatment. Tumults and brawls broke out. The pope reacted to these scandalous proceedings with excommunication and interdict, which were common ecclesiastical punishments at the time.

Why had Br. Elias and the city officials cooperated in this affair when the angry reaction of those they intended to exclude could easily have been forseen? The explanation lies in the mediaeval way of thinking. For a mediaeval city, it was very important to have the relics of a saint within its walls. This was not only a question of drawing a large number of pilgrims, which — then as now — would be a significant financial factor. In a way that frequently bordered on the magical, one expected an almost automatic protection from misfortune and from the attacks of enemies because of the presence of the relics. Frequently cities would compete with one another for the relics of the greatest saints. And Assisi could well be concerned that its rival city, Perugia, would try to gain possession of the relics of Francis. For this reason, the civil authorities of the city of Assisi wished to insure the safety of these precious relics. This was done by burying them in an unknown place and protecting them with a strong wall. Basically, the civil authorities and Br. Elias wished to perform a worthwhile service to the city of Assisi. This was certainly one reason why the mantle of forgiveness was soon spread over these unpleasant events.

Anthony had come to the general chapter at Assisi to ask the minister general, John Parenti, to free him from the burden of the office of minister provincial. He had serious reasons for this. His health was not the best. Also, he wished to give more attention to the growing pastoral needs of Padua and the surrounding region. He sensed that he needed a more peaceful rhythm in his work. He was successful with his request to be relieved of office.

The General Chapter of May 25, 1230

It was not only the tumultuous proceedings surrounding the final burial of the relics of Francis that burdened the general chapter at Assisi. There were difficult conflicts within the chapter, which at times became quite stormy. Four years after the death of St. Francis, the spiritual nature of the Order was at stake. This was one of the most important and influential general chapters of the Order. Through the charism of St. Francis, the Rule approved by the pope in 1223 had become an eminent document of spiritual principles. But it contained juridical and institutional elements as well. However, these were neither extensive nor detailed. In the course of the seven years during which the Order had followed this Rule, a number of uncertainties had arisen concerning the practical interpretation of particular points of the Rule.

As is always the case in such situations, there was a wide range of viewpoints and opinions. Today we would call those representing the widest extremes progressives and conservatives, an evaluation that is made from our own particular stand-point. At that time, there were brothers for whom the beginning of the Order with its radical approach particularly to the question of poverty represented the ideal which, under any circumstances, was to be preserved in its original form. These friars were supported by the aging companions of St. Francis who spoke enthusiastically of the glorious beginnings of the Order. They wished to remain faithful to the old ideals. But they did not always distinguish between the ideal and the forms in which the ideal was expressed. Such forms need to be constantly created anew. Who could think ill of them for wanting to hold to the "good old times" and for glorifying the past? This happens in any community that has a past to look to.

On the other hand, there were brothers who wished to deal with the enormous numerical growth of the Order. Was is possible to take a life-style that had been possible for a small, homogeneous group and now impose it on an Order that numbered several thousand brothers and was spread over a number of nations. Naturally it would be possible to deal with this situation only if one were willing to depart from the enthusiasm and radical nature of the earlier times and make some compromises with human weakness. These were brothers who also were edified by the accounts of the "good old times," but were convinced that these good old times could not be restored and already belonged to history.

Even though the two groups were hardly aware of it, they shared a common concern at least on one point. They viewed the matters of the Rule as a collection of legal prescriptions whose observance or non-observance could be juridically determined. In this context, even the Testament of St. Francis was discussed in the deliberations of the chapter. Here the question was whether the Testament of the saint was "binding" or "non-binding" for the Order. "Binding" was taken in the sense of "legally binding." The fact that there might be a spiritual obligation that lay at a deeper level than that which is "legally binding" seemed hardly to be recognized.

Anthony attempted to act as a mediator in the affairs

of the chapter, but to no avail. The minister general, John Parenti, was not in control of things. It is said that he possessed the gift of tears, which was highly treasured in the Middle Ages. It may, indeed, be a precious quality to react in such a strongly emotional way; but for an Order that needed to establish its institutional foundation, the gift of tears was certainly not the necessary disposition to provide effective leadership for the Order. Without doubt, Br. John Parenti was kind and intelligent, but he was already advanced in age and was incapable of leading the chapter effectively. Often he even made matters worse by intervening in issues that were already complex enough.

The general chapter was unable to arrive at a compromise which all could accept. A way out of the impasse was found by appealing to the pope for a decision. The Rule of the Order from 1223 had been confirmed by a document of Pope Honorius III. What has been established by a pope can subsequently be validly interpreted by a pope. So the chapter-assembly decided to ask the pope for an authoritative explanation of the debated points from the Rule and the Testament of Francis. The pope was Gregory IX who, as Cardinal Hugolino, had helped St. Francis in many difficult questions and had played a role in the final redaction of the Rule.

As a Deputy of the General Chapter in Rome

The general chapter appointed a commission whose task was to present the debated questions of the Order to the pope for a decision. On this commission were the following: Haymo of Faversham (later minister general of the Order), Gerhard Rossignol (papal penitentiary), Leone (later archbishop of Milan), Gerhard of Modena, Peter of Brescia, the minister general of the Order, John Parenti — and Anthony of Padua. The fact that Anthony was appointed to this commission even though he had relinquished his office as provincial indicates the great trust which his confrerers must have had in him.

It is possible to identify the problems which Anthony and the commission appointed by the general chapter brought to the pope by looking at the pope's response which was given on September 28, 1230, in the bull "Quo elongati." This document, by its very nature, is a strictly juridical treatment and must be read as such. Together with other matters, the following points are settled:

The Testament is not a juridically binding norm.

The brothers are not held to the observance of all the counsels of the Gospel. They are obliged to observe only those counsels to which they are bound by virtue of the Rule of the Order.

At the request of the brothers, the ban against money is not removed. But measures were taken to see that money which was given for the brothers could be used for them, even though they had no control over the use of such money.

The poverty of the Order as a whole, as well as that of the individual brothers, is to be maintained.

Examination and approval for the office of preaching is reserved to the minister general. This holds only for those who appear to be in need of such examination.

Together with the minister general, the minister provincial is responsible for the reception of new brothers.

Provincial ministers have the right to participate in the general chapters. Also, one of the custodies of the particular province may participate in the general chapters.

Anthony had taken neither of the extreme positions. He had attempted to be a mediator at the chapter because he was convinced that only a middle position was possible if the Order was to grow and work effectively within the church. Papal decisions and later developments in the Order show that his viewpoint was right.

VI.
THE LAST PERIOD OF HIS LIFE IN PADUA

It was between the end of 1227 and the beginning of 1228 that Anthony first came to Padua. The brothers of St. Francis had arrived in Padua already in the year 1217. Near the city in a place called Arcella, a convent of Poor Clares had been established. A small friary of the brothers was connected with it to provide for the pastoral care of the Poor Clares. When Anthony arrived at Padua, he went to this small friary.

At that time, the blessed Helena Enselmini lived in the Poor Clare cloister of Arcella. She died on November 4, 1242 (1230?). Unfortunately, we have no specific information about any contact between St. Anthony and this mystic.

In Padua, he also met his confrere, the blessed Luke Belludi, who had been a faithful friend. Luke, who died after July 9, 1285, in Padua, was the provincial who would later provide for the rich adornment of the basilica dedicated to the Saint. Luke's grave is found in the Basilica of St. Anthony in the "Capella del beato Luca Belludi," named after him.

It is to Brother Luke Belludi that we must attribute the close connection between Anthony and Padua. Anthony was, so to say, introduced to Padua by Luke. This young friar came from a wealthy family which, naturally, had significant influence. He had an outstanding education and influential relations.

Very important for Anthony's work was the good friendship of the Benedictine Abbot, Jordan Forzate, a man held generally in high esteem. It is certain that Anthony's visit to Padua in 1227-1228 had not been very lengthy. But some sort of spark must have been struck so that, toward the end of his life, the Saint was drawn back here. Several years earlier, he had written his collection of Sunday sermons for the church-year there. Now after he had given up the office of provincial, he began working out sermons for feast-days.

The *Legenda Assidua* records the following about the final phase of the Saint's life: "Since he had already stayed at Padua at an earlier time, namely, when he wrote his Sunday sermons for the church-year, he decided to return there after he had been freed from the offices of the Order. After he had come to Padua under divine impulse, he interrupted his preaching activity and devoted himself for the entire winter to the study of Christian moral teaching. At the wish of the Cardinal of Ostia, he began writing sermons for the feast-days of the church-year. After the servant of God, Anthony, had thus put himself at the service of the salvation of his fellow human beings, the Lenten Season was at hand. Then, as he saw the time of grace and the days of salvation to be close at hand, he laid his work aside and gave himself fully to the task of preaching to the people who were so desirous of salvation."

Always Challenged Anew

From 1228 onward, Anthony had maintained his own permanent place of residence in Padua. But his obligations as provincial and as a missionary preacher made it necessary for him to be perpetually on the road. If it would be proper to say that the whole world had been his place of work with constantly changing stages, from 1230 onward he concentrated his concerns on Padua. Surely he had a great personal interest in finishing the series of feast-day sermons on which he was working. But he never made it a maxim of his life to give absolute priority to his own personal desires.

Anthony's life was basically like the life that the Gospels depict in the case of Jesus and the Apostles. The Apostles had returned from their first mission. They had given themselves generously to the preaching of the King-dom of God and to care for the poor and the sick. And now they needed rest. Jesus saw this clearly. So He said: "Come away by yourselves to a lonely place, and rest a while." But when they had arrived by boat at the place where they had hoped to rest, there was a great throng of people there waiting for instruction and assistance. And Jesus responded to them again (cf. Mk 6:30-35).

This is the way it was with Anthony. Padua was the place where he wished to rest and to find more quiet than he had been able to find previously. Certainly the desire to work out his series of sermons was also a motivating factor. And surely, after all the strenuous activity he had been engaged in, he felt his energies declining. At the beginning of the final period of his life, at Padua, he continued his preaching activity, but limited it somewhat. For the most part, he preached in the church of Santa Maria connected with his convent, but he preached also in other churches of Padua. From the beginning of the winter of 1230 until Lent of 1231, in recollection and quiet, he worked on the sermon-outlines for the feast-days of the church-year until he saw himself called again to the work of preaching.

The Lofty Mission of the Preacher

The *Legenda Assidua*, which we have already men-tioned, makes it clear that Anthony gave himself with renewed intensity to preaching during the Lent of 1231.

During this time of grace and salvation, he saw it as his undeniable obligation to proclaim to the people the Good News of the Kingdom and the mercy of God. We can discover his real motivation for this from his own words: "The Lord, whose mercy knows no limits, calls his people not only by himself; he does it also through his preachers. For this reason it is said in the Gospel (Lk 14:17): 'He sent his servant to say to those who had been invited, come; for all is now ready.' And the Glossa (the **Glossa ordinaria**) comments on this: 'The hour of the meal is the end of the ages.' Therefore the Apostle writes (1 Cor 10:11): it is we 'upon whom the end of the ages had come.' At this end of the ages, the Lord sends his servant, that is, his preachers, to those whom he has invited through the Law and the prophets. They should be free from excess so that they can enjoy the meal, for everything is prepared. After the sacrifice of Christ, the gate to the Kingdom of God is open. The suffering of Christ has opened the gate to the Kingdom of heaven so that the church or the just might enter for the first meal, and even for the second meal."

We have no concrete evidence of the thoughts which Anthony presented in the sermons of the Lenten period of 1231. But the thoughts just presented indicate how seriously he took the task of the preacher. He saw this task above all as one through which human beings should be called to the merciful love of God who desires to invite people into the Kingdom of God and into a beatifying communion with God through the sacrifice of Christ. Precisely this message belongs in the center of preaching during the pre-Easter preparation for the feast that commemorates our redemption.

In the Service of the Sacrament of Reconciliation

Anthony did not limit his pastoral service to preaching in this final pre-Easter penitential season of his life, even though this apostolate demanded the fullness of his powers since he gave himself to it fully. As at other times, he gave much time and pastoral care to the sacrament of reconciliation. Early in the morning, he was ready in the confessional; and he was found there until sunset. For him, the sermon and confession were related to each other. We can see this in the following words taken from one of his sermons:

"A leper came and knelt before him (Mt 8:2ff). Behold in this the humble confession of sins. Even more explicit is Mark (1:40): 'A leper came to him beseeching him, and kneeling said to him: if you will, you can make me clean.' So the sinner who comes to confession should kneel before the priest who represents God, for the priest has from Christ the power to bind and to loose. The sinner ought to have so firm a faith in this power that he too will say: 'Lord, if you will you can make me clean and free me from my sins.' 'And immediately the leprosy left him, and he was made clean.' Through his priests, the Lord repeats this daily in the heart of the sinner, for the priest must do three things: he must stretch out his hand, touch, and will. He reaches out his hand when he prays to God for the sinner and is moved with compassion for him. He touches the sinner when he comforts him with the promise of God's forgiveness. He has the will to make him clean when he pronounces the words of absolution."

Anthony speaks of the mystery of confession in strikingly clear words. Are there many people who are concerned that the secret of confession might not be properly observed? The words of the Saint on this point ought to relieve any sinner of the fear that something from his confession could become known to others:

"The confession of the sinner must be inaccessible to anyone else, for it takes place in the presence of four eyes, it is secret, it is hidden from all other human knowledge, and it is closed up in the memory of the priest as in a treasury with an unbreakable seal. It is sealed in such a way that you must conceal the sins of your penitent and protect them with the seal of eternal silence even if everyone else in the world knows of them. Indeed, they are sons of Satan, cursed by the true and living God, rejected by the church triumphant, and expelled from the church militant, forfeit of their office and pastoral role — those who betray or reveal a confession — I do not say by words, for that would be worse than death —, but even by a sign or in any way through laughter or a nod of the head. I will be entirely open about it: Anyone who reveals a confession sins more seriously than did Judas, the traitor, who betrayed the Son of God to the Jews."

In these words we see that Anthony not only encouraged the faithful to receive the sacrament of penance, but he also attempted in a clever psychological way to remove the obstacles which might keep people from doing so. A good preacher relies not only on knowledge of dogmatic and moral theology. He must also attempt in an intelligent way to remove obstacles. Precisely here we can sense something of the mysterious success which Anthony had with his sermons.

It is said that after his sermons, the many priests present were not sufficient for the task of hearing the confessions of all those who wanted to receive the sacrament. In this we can recognize the power of the faith renewed by Anthony. For at that time, the reception of the sacrament of penance had in general become more difficult since the Waldensians openly campaigned against confession to a priest. Hence, the great rush to confession was simultaneously a unique sort of faith-confession.

The Miracle of the Restored Foot

One particular detail from this confessional ministry is given to us in a tradition. A young man from Padua had confessed to Anthony that he had given his mother a good kick. Anthony rebuked him sharply and told him that the foot which had done such a thing deserved to be cut off. No doubt he was thinking of the words of Jesus: "And if your hand or your foot causes you to sin, cut it off and throw it away; it is better for you to enter life maimed or lame than with two hands or two feet to be thrown into the eternal fire" (Mt 18:8). The young man was so shocked that he followed this saying quite literally and actually cut off his foot with an axe. This was reported to Anthony. Immediately he hurried to the house of the young man and restored the foot. This affair gained considerable attention later. Donatello depicted it in bronze, and Tullio Lombardo did the same in marble.

Here we see a stage in the formation of the pious tradition about Anthony which occurs frequently in mediaeval lives of the saints: a text of Holy Scripture which the Saint had used with convincing power is confirmed and concretely illustrated by means of a miracle.

Anthony Becomes Anthony of Padua

Apparently it was the energetic work of the Saint in this Lenten period of 1231 that made Anthony into "Anthony of Padua." What took place in Padua at that time is best described in the superlative, even without any exaggerated, legendary descriptions or interpretations. Anthony held his carefully prepared Lenten sermons from February 6 till March 23, 1231. He was the first one who prepared for the feast of Easter by preaching daily. This would later become a common practise.

From the beginning, there was a great stream of people who wished to hear Anthony. This was remarkable, since he was not an amusing entertainer. On the contrary, he was a man who went clearly and unambiguously to the matter at hand and challenged his listeners in the name of God. The number of listeners increased from day to day. None of the churches of Padua chosen for the sermons — for a church seemed to be the fitting place for a sermon — was large enough to hold the throng of the faithful. Finally, it was decided to hold them in a large open place; and an appropriate pulpit was erected for the preacher. According to the oldest Legenda of Anthony, the number of listeners on many days was estimated at 30,000. This number may well be exaggerated out of enthusiasm, but even the exaggeration indicates that the flood of people was immense.

Many people gathered at the site of the sermon already during the night in order to assure themselves of a good place. Anyone who was free to do so would come to the sermon: old and young, men and women, and even soldiers. It must have been like a pilgrimage to a holy place when the important and highly respected people of the city arrived at the site of the sermon: the bishop at the head, followed by the diocesan clergy, then the Franciscan friars and members of other orders, the professors and the students. Nobles came as well as artisans and merchants. A Sunday rest prevailed in the city during the time of the sermon. Businesses were closed, and merchants from the market place — who profited much from the crowds of people — left their stands.

But, as things usually go, the limits of piety proper to such occasions were not observed. There were incidents which may have seemed pious to certain people, but which in reality were an awkward and embarrassing burden for the preacher. Apparently Anthony was considered a sort of relic already during his life, and people wished to get some sort of article belonging to him. Moved by pious enthusiasm, women came to the sermons with scissors and cut little pieces from the habit of the Saint as he passed through the crowds to the pulpit.

In order to put a stop to this embarrassing annoyance

and to avoid the necessity of Anthony preaching in a habit that was cut and full of holes, a sort of body-guard of young men was formed. They opened a way for him through the crowd and took care that he could get to and from the pulpit unmolested.

A powerful wave of moral conversion moved through Padua. This was not a conversion that sought reconciliation only with God and believed that, given such a conversion, one could ignore one's neighbor. Anthony had always made it clear that reconciliation with God had to manifest itself in reconciliation with one's neighbor:

"As great and even greater than the difference between ten-thousand talents and a hundred denarii (Mt 18:24ff) is the difference between the sin by which we injure God and that by which we injure our fellow human being. If God forgives such great guilt in his creatures, why will you not forgive the much smaller guilt in your neighbor? He who forgets what great mercy he has received does not have a heart full of mercy for others."

Through his sermons, Anthony brought great crowds of people to the sacrament of penance. He also brought them to reconciliation with one another and to a proper sort of human relation. At that time Padua experienced a period in which the citizens were ready to live at peace with one another. There was a desire for the good that embraced wide circles. People at odds with one another extended their hands in reconciliation and buried their differences. Property that had been unjustly acquired was returned. Prisoners were freed. In this instance, we must keep in mind that this was not a question of criminals, but of people who, because of unfortunate circumstances, were unable to pay their debts. Thieves and prostitutes turned from their former ways and began a new life in decency. It could be said that the people of Padua experienced, in a holy intoxication, that they could live a life according to the Gospel in peace with God and with their human brothers and sisters.

The Law of March 15, 1231

Toward the end of the Lenten season, the work of St. Anthony found expression in the form of a law of wide social significance. It had to do with the practise of the usurers and the operative norms for loaning money. At this time, the laws of the city of Padua and of other cities punished debtors and their guarantors with imprisonment for life, and made no distinction between those who were unable to pay and those who were unwilling to pay. On March 15, 1231, the city authorities enacted a new law which stated the following: "At the request of the venerable and holy brother, Anthony, the confessor of the Order of Friars Minor, no one, whether a debtor or a guarantor, is to be deprived of his personal freedom in the future if he is incapable of paying. In such a case, he can be deprived of his property, but not of his personal freedom."

This law is certainly unique since it is inspired by a man who had no political power of any sort and who did not have the support of any particular special-interest groups. In the case of Anthony, it was solely a question of spiritual authority and the authority of the word of God which he proclaimed. It was to this alone that he wished to appeal and did, in fact, appeal.

This law of March 15, 1231, cleaned up a lot of evil that had developed not only in the city of Padua but in the surrounding territory. Power and wealth had grown in the cities and were closely allied with each other. This arrangement allowed the development of the economy and the power structures to reach a high-point and enhanced the self-image of the civil authorities of the cities. Here lay the threatening seeds of unhealthy controversies.

The cities had always known rivalries between the outstanding and influential families as well as tension between these families and the simple people who had no influence. The development of a money-based economy sharpened the old problems and created new ones. While one group had an abundance of money, the other group lacked money and amounted to an oppressed, urban proletariat. Clever business people who saw an opportunity for themselves in the monetary needs of others opened lending banks. Because of their interest rates, these brought many people into debt and led to hopeless misery. For anyone who could not pay back the borrowed money together with the interest, or anyone who had declared himself incapable of payment, was imprisoned at the request of the banker, much as we recognize the situation in Jesus' parable of the merciless servant (cf. Mt 18:23-35).

Through his intervention, Anthony succeeded in changing this unjust situation at least in Padua despite the fact that the wealthy could well have believed that they were in the right and should be allowed to press their claims against the weak. This legal reform is not counted among the miracles of the Saint, even though it may well be the greatest of the miracles which he worked during his life-time. Human faith in miracles associates other sorts of things with the miraculous.

Miraculous Occurrences

It would have been unthinkable for the Legenda that Anthony would perform no miraculous deeds in the city of Padua, whose name finally came to be associated with him. Indeed, a number of outstanding occurrences had been reserved for Padua. But here something remarkable emerges. With the exception of the healing of a three-year-old girl who was lame and who suffered from epilepsy, the miracles associated with his time in Padua are related to the Saint's family in far-away Portugal. It is as though precisely when Padua wanted to claim him for itself, his home-land likewise laid claim to him.

Bartholomew Albizzi of Pisa, also known as Bartholomew of Pisa, in a work that speaks of the "Likeness of the Life of St. Francis with the Life of the Lord Jesus," tells of two instances of bilocation. The work appeared around 1385, a time in which the stories of Anthony's miracles had developed extensively. In a somewhat uncritical way, the author gathered together everything that came to his attention.

Thus he tells of a noble man in Lisbon who was murdered by a rival. In an attempt to give misleading clues, the killer secretly buried the corpse in the garden of St. Anthony's family. Then, in a cunning way, he saw to it that the body would be found there. Naturally the family was accused and brought to trial. But the family had the best lawyer available. For Anthony, who was living in distant Padua, appeared at the trial in Lisbon. He called the dead man back to life and drew from him a statement which freed the relatives of the Saint from all guilt and suspicion. In a second instance, Anthony was experienced both in Padua and in Lisbon where he came to the assistance of his father, Martin. The king had transferred some property to Martin to administer. When the time of his responsibility was over, he returned all that had been given to him together with the profits he had made. But he made a mistake which was to have disastrous effects in the jungle of intrigue and machinations at the royal court. He had not taken care to make sure that he could prove he had returned the goods which had been entrusted to him. His enemies took advantage of this fact and demanded that he pay back the goods a second time. Anthony, ready to come to the aid of his father, appeared in Lisbon, threatened the deceivers with a harsh punishment from God, and forced them to produce a receipt for the goods they had received.

We should not be annoyed with people who have doubts about these accounts of bilocation or who reject them. We have no reliable sources to determine whether the parents of the Saint were still living or whether they had died. It is noteworthy, however, that from the time of the Saint's entrance into the Augustinian convent a Coimbra, nothing more is said of his parents in the sources of his life-story. It was only toward the end of the fourteenth century that the tradition of the legends speak again of his parents. It is impossible to determine today whether there were any genuine events involved here. It is significant for the tradition about the Saint, however, that apparently impossible things are attributed to Anthony. Thus, these accounts may tell us more about the cult of the Saint than about his actual life.

The Tyrant Ezzelino da Romano

The spectacular encounter between Anthony and Ezzelino da Romano (1194-1259) has won special attention in accounts of his life and works. If anyone from that period of history deserved the unpleasant title "tyrant," it was this man. He was the leader of the Ghibellines, the party of the emperor in Italy. He saw it as his task to gain control over the cities of the opposing party, the Guelphs, as well as over the free cities. As a brilliant military leader, he went about this in a truly gruesome and blood-thirsty way. Many of his contemporaries saw him as a monster from hell.

Ezzelino made his camp at Verona. Before him, the Counts of Sambonifacio had ruled, the most important of which was Ricardo, whose sister had become the wife of Ezzelino. But Ezzelino succeeded in excluding his brother-in-law from the struggle for power and took over the rule of Verona in 1226. His brother, Alberich, succeeded in gaining control of Vicenza. This concentration of power in the hands of the notorious Ezzelini alarmed the cities of northern Italy. As a protective alliance, Padua, Milan, Bologna, Brescia, Mantua, Vicenza, and Treviso joined the League of Lombard. It is because of the influence of this League that the two Ezzelini were forced to relinquish their power in Verona and Vicenza when their terms of office had run out.

In Verona, the Counts of Sambonifacio returned, with Richard now at the head. They were supported by the league of cities and by the house of Este. But Ezzelino succeeded in getting the family of the Monticoli's in Verona to rebel against the family of the Sambonifacio's and to set up one of their own people as ruler of the city. Even though Riccardo was his brother-in-law, the tyrant captured him and his followers in a sly maneuver on June 27, 1230. They were thrown into Ezzelino's dungeon, which was unfortunately well-known.

Some Guelphs from Verona who had escaped the gruesome action of Ezzelino found refuge in Padua. They hoped in Padua to find help and mediation for the release of their imprisoned relatives by means of the League of the Lombard cities. But it was really too much for Padua. Certainly the leaders of Padua wanted to help; but how could they deal with the cruel, cunning Ezzelino? A military solution was unthinkable. In view of the military genius of Ezzelino and the great distance between Padua and Verona, such an action would have been pointless from the start.

After much discussion, the leaders of Padua believed they saw a way that could succeed. It was the Abbot Jordan Forzate, a friend of St. Anthony, who suggested the idea that Padua should send to Verona a man who enjoyed the greatest personal authority. This man would ask Ezzelino for clemency. It was known that Ezzelino could be generous in negotiations if he could gain something from it for himself. Anthony was selected to undertake this difficult mission. It was hoped that Ezzelino would not close himself to this man who was already recognized for his saintliness.

Even though the difficulty of this undertaking was clear to him, Anthony did not reject the request. So he made the trip to Verona. But he did not go directly to Ezzelino. Instead, he tried to get some information in the region about the prospects for his mission and about the best way of approaching Ezzelino. So he sought the advice of the leaders of the Lombard League and even spoke with the advisors of the tyrant. But he did not have the slightest bit of success with Ezzelino. The spiritual authority of the Saint did not make the slightest impression, and the words of the Gospel bounced off of his hard heart. Anthony experienced a complete failure. He was fortunate that he was allowed to return home with no threat to his life and health.

Only after another four months, upon the request of a leader from Padua, was Ezzelino ready to free the imprisoned Riccardo. In 1232, the tyrant allied himself closely with the emperor, Frederick II, who gave him his daughter, Selvaggia, as his wife. The emperor turned over the rule of the cities of Vicenza, Treviso, and Padua to Ezzelino; and the cities soon experienced his wrath. Because of his notorious cruelty, he was excommunicated by the pope; but he was hardly impressed by the fact. Neither was he impressed when an army of crusaders under the leadership of the archbishop of Ravenna attacked him. He defeated the crusaders in the battle of Torricella on September 1, 1258.

But his fate finally overtook him when he was wounded in the battle of Soncino on September 27, 1259, and wound up a prisoner in Milan. A few days later, on October 1, 1259, he died. How we would like to know what an impression it made on Ezzelino when the Anthony whose appeal he had rejected was canonized on May 30, 1232. But we have no information about this.

Anthony had experienced a painful disappointment at the hands of Ezzelino. He had accomplished nothing. But the later authors of the Legends did not accept that. The Saint whom they honored would have had to be successful at all times. Thus, they depict Ezzelino as a man who was changed by the preachings of the Saint from destructive wolfe to a harmless, peaceful lamb. This led even to paintings which depict an Ezzelino who declares himself ready for conversion as he throws himself at the feet of St. Anthony with a penitential cord around his neck. It would have been nice if it had worked out this way; but it did not.

Anthony certainly suffered from the frustration of his mission. But it was not the grief of a wounded pride that could accept no opposition. Rather, it was the pain of seeing the proclamation of Christ's message of peace come to nothing against the hard heart of a powerful man who was in a position to create peace. Again he experienced how the power of evil resists the Gospel, an experience which he had often enough in the past, particularly in the form of personal accusations and denunciations.

VII.
RETURN HOME
TO THE LORD

During his second stay at Padua, Anthony lived at the cloister of the friars near the church of Sancta Maria Mater Domini. The basilica dedicated to the Saint stands on this spot today. After his return from Verona, Anthony stayed there only a short time. The trip to Verona had sapped his already declining strength even more. He was tired and desired rest. With the approach of summer, it was not advisable to remain in the city where the sultry heat would have made any recovery impossible. For this reason, he wished to go to a country place at Camposampiero.

Final Rest in Camposampiero

About eighteen kilometers from Padua there lies Camposampiero where a faithful friend and generous benefactor of Anthony and his confreres, Count Tiso VI, had a castle, on the grounds of which he had provided a chapel and a hermitage for the friars.

There Anthony found what he was looking for: quiet and isolation so that he could give himself intensively to prayer and contemplation of God. It was no longer a question of bodily recovery or the creation of new strength. It was certainly too late for that. Anthony was suffering from dropsy and asthma. Modern medical doctors who have studied the testimony of the early descriptions of his life with a view to a possible diagnosis have come to the conclusion that Anthony could have suffered from diabetes. It is impossible for us today to come to an exact diagnosis of his illness.

Even though the land of Count Tiso could provide relaxation and joy, there still remained the painful nights for a man suffering from dropsy and asthma who could find no sleep as he turned from side to side.

The Cell in the Walnut Tree

On the property of Count Tiso there was a large walnut tree with wide-spreading branches. We do not know who came up with the idea of building a sort of "cell" or — better — a "nest" in this tree, but Count Tiso saw to it that a hut that resembled a nest was built for Anthony in the branches of the tree. Anthony was glad to withdraw to this place.

What could move a man who was a saint to choose a nest at the top of a walnut tree as his residence? He could find silence and isolation in other ways. Was it an attempt to experience the Franciscan unity with nature there in the branches where the leaves moved to the slightest breeze? Experiencing a tree in the fullness of its life from within the embrace of its branches is quite different from viewing a tree from a distance on the ground.

Climbing up into the tree and dwelling in its height can also be seen as a sort of symbol for the final days of the Saint on earth. He begins to set aside the lower concerns of earthly life and activity. He strives for the higher, that which is above. But in this, he is surrounded by and supported by the powers of the natural world created by God and by its living richness.

The Vision of the Child Jesus

Anthony had given aid to many people, often in a miraculous way. Now toward the end of his days on earth, God gave him an experience which was for himself alone, and was to offer him consolation and joy in the distress of his illness. As the Legenda informs us, Jesus appeared to him in the form of a child, allowed Anthony to embrace him, and touched the Saint on the forehead. According to the Legenda, there was a witness to this event. At this precise moment, Count Tiso was passing by the cell of the Saint. He saw a light shining from the room and entered it. Perhaps he wanted to offer some companionshiip to his sleepless friend. Was the light perhaps so bright that the Count assumed a fire had broken out and came to be of assistance? In any case, he witnessed the miraculous occurrence. Deeply touched, he fell to his knees.

When the appearance came to an end, Anthony saw the Count kneeling at the open door. Anthony recognized that the heavenly apparition had not remained his personal secret, but he did not complain to the Count. He had not forced himself into the Saint's secret out of curiosity but had been drawn by concern for Anthony. The Saint asked the Count to promise that he would not reveal what he had seen. After the death of the Saint, Count Tiso no longer felt bound by the promise of silence and made the miracle known to others.

Appearances of the Child Jesus are narrated in the case of other saints. It is called a "wandering legend."Is It then possible that this did not really happen to Anthony? Whatever the case may be, the fact that such an account has been associated with Anthony has deeper roots in the teaching of this doctor of the church. In his sermons, he gave a central significance to the incarnation of the eternal Son of god. In this sense, the appearance of the Child Jesus has an inner justification and stands as a statement about Anthony. The same can be said of the later depictions which show Anthony with the Christ Child on his arm.

Remnants in Camposampiero

Over the centuries, the castle of Count Tiso has totally disappeared. The tiny, ancient church dedicated to St. John as well as the friary at Camposampiero have been altered and renovated many times.

But despite all the changes and renovations, the cell of St. Anthony has been preserved. It was a small room, 4.20 meters long and 2.65 meters wide. The walls are of unplastered stone. Formerly a narrow door led to the corridor of the ancient cloister. Today this door is covered over. A dormer and a small window allowed a view of the park surrounding the castle. On the wall a picture of Anthony hangs. His face is pale and somewhat bloated. In his hands he holds a lily and a book, symbols of purity and wisdom. The board on which this image is painted is said to be the place where Anthony rested. In its present state, it shows signs of the enduring veneration of the Saint, and it has suffered much under the pressure of this veneration. For many of the faithful have tried to demonstrate their piety by cutting pieces from the board so that they could take a relic home with them.

The ancient walnut tree no longer exists. But it has reproduced itself in many other trees. These have a distinctive peculiarity that makes them exceptional among walnut trees. They always grow their leaves during the novena that precedes the feast of Anthony. In 1432, a descendant of Count Tiso had a small church built on the spot where the old wanut tree had stood. It is known as "St. Anthony of the Walnut Tree."

A Life Rich in Work Comes to an End

There is a prayer to the Mother of God contained in Anthony's sermons which reveals his peaceful, confident attitude toward death: "We ask you, our Lady, our hope, be a light for us in our distress, a star on the stormy sea. Lead us to a safe harbor. With your presence, protect us in death so that we may, with confidence, leave the prison of the body and arrive at inexpressible joy." It is certainly not wrong to assume that images such as "stormy sea," "star of the sea," "safe harbor" as metaphors for human life have their source in a personal experience. Anthony may have been thinking of the frightful storm which had driven him from Morocco to Sicily.

His stay at Camposampiero lasted only a few weeks. "Brother Death" — or more precisely according to the Italian of Francis' Canticle, "Sister Death" — arrived on the evening of June 13, 1231, to take Anthony home to the harbor of eternity. It was a Friday. Did Anthony sense the nearness of his death and perhaps predict it in a hidden way? Many biographers draw this conclusion from the following incident. When Anthony had arrived at the heights of the mountains on his return from Verona, he looked down upon the city of Padua which was so beloved to him. There he is supposed to have said to the brothers who accompanied him that, in a short time, Padua would experience a great honor. This has been interpreted to mean that Padua would preserve the relics of Anthony within its walls. For nothing else seems to have happened in "a short time" that could be considered a great honor.

As on every day, the friary bell rang on June 13, 1231, to call the brothers at Camposampiero together for the noon-day meal. Wearily, Anthony climbed down from his cell in the tree to go to the friary. He found it ever more difficult to walk since disturbances in his metabolism had caused him to become somewhat corpulent. Old paintings that have been untouched depict him this way. Many painters later depict him as a handsome, slim young man. Corpulence does not seem to be edifying.

Anthony had hardly sat down to begin the meal when Brother Death announced his presence. Could it have been a stroke? Suddenly he felt very ill.His face became as pale as a corpse. His head sank to his chest. He lost his strength. He knew that his end was near. He had still one wish. He requested that he be brought to the friary at Padua near the church of Sancta Maria Mater Domini. The brothers at Camposampiero would gladly have kept him with them, but they respected the wish of the dying man. So they set out on a sad journey, which was poor in every respect. From a farmer the brothers borrowed a cart drawn by two oxen. The only comfort for the dying man was the bundles of brush-wood laid on the floor of the cart. Br. Luke Belludi and Br. Roger accompanied him. The journey followed the ancient Roman road known today as the "Road of the Saint." Because of the condition of the mortally sick man, the journey went very slowly. In oppressive heat, the cart bumped along on the stone road. This agonizing journey may have lasted about five or six hours.

By evening, they had reached Arcella at the edge of Padua. There Br. Vinotto met the sad procession. Because of the dire condition of the dying man, Br. Vinotto advised them to stop at the small house of the brothers near the Poor Clares at Arcella. Did the possibility of obtaining the precious relics of Anthony play a role already at this point? This is cetainly not impossible if the mediaeval mind-set is taken into account. We saw this already in the events surrounding the burial of St. Francis.

Anthony agreed to stop at Arcella. Was he thinking of the way in which people had cut pieces from his habit during the Lenten sermons? At that time, a group of young men had protected him. What would happen now if he were drawn slowly through the streets of Padua on the cart. It is possible that he feared the pressing throngs that were to be expected and preferred to remain in Arcella. Also, he sensed that his final hour had come.

Anthony, placed in bed in the house of the brothers, seemed to be losing consciousness. He asked for the anointing of the sick, which in this case could rightly be called the "last anointing." In accordance with the customary rites for the dying, the brothers prayed the seven penitential psalms. The dying man followed the prayers in concentrated devotion. Then a change came over him. His eyes lit up. And he said: "I see my Lord." After these words, he passed into the eternal vision of the Lord, in whose service he had used all his strength.

His death was announced to the citizens of Padua in a remarkable manner. The children of Padua became restless. They ran through the streets and called out: "The Saint has died! The holy father has died!" No one had told the children this or had given them any sort of indication.

The Fight For the Body

For us today, the events that took place between the death of St. Anthony on the evening of June 13, 1231, and his burial on June 17, 1231, are quite unbelievable. Two factors were involved which make it difficult for us to grasp what happened at that time. First, there was the Italian temperament which is very spontaneous when it comes to the veneration of the saints and can literally explode, unlike the temperament of Germans whose reaction is held back by caution and reserve. And then, it must be kept in mind that these were mediaeval people who were often driven by a massive and at times almost magical confidence in the relics of the saints. The relics of saints were seen as a power which could play a role even in political struggles for power. It was for this reason that Assisi had brought Francis home in his final sickness, taking a wide detour around Perugia and accompanying him with a military escort. Likewise Assisi had hidden the relics of Francis in the church that served as his monument and had made them very difficult to reach. It was feared that the powerful, rival city, Perugia, could take the precious treasure of Francis away from Assisi, which was a smaller city.

"Unbelievable but true." This describes well the events that took place between the death and the burial of St. Anthony. In dealing with many events of Anthony's lifetime, it has been necessary to depend on guesses which can be helpful to some degree. But good and detailed documentary material exists for the events which we have to describe now. P. Scandaletti has used this material for his biography of Anthony which appeared in the German translation with the title: *Antonius von Padua, Volksheiliger und Kirchenlehrer* (Styria-Verlag). The following text is taken from pages 158-163 of this book. It will be noted that at times Scandaletti turns the friars into "monks," a title which belongs properly only to the monastic orders:

"The oldest chronicler of Anthony's life was the first to give the following testimony, which occurs expressly in the second part of his book. The anonymous author of the *Assidua* claims that 'he writes with humble veneration, but after he had arrived at an image that was true to reality,' and about 'wondrous matters' which 'have been related to us through the accounts of trustworthy people.'

Accordingly, Anthony had hardly died when many problems arose. It started out badly for his confreres: they wished to keep his death a secret, but the news of it spread through the entire city with the speed of the wind. As usually happens, someone gave it away, despite protestations to the contrary . . . Many hurried to the cloister. Some wanted to confirm the news for themselves. Others, out of a sense of devotion, wanted to see the Saint for a last time and perhaps to get a piece of his habit to take home as a relic. For several days, those who were less lucky but more clever had the idea of bringing personal possessions in order to touch them to the body of the Saint.

To this mixture of religiosity and primitive fanaticism must be added the unrestrained interests of the Poor Clares, the people living in the neighborhood, as well as the friars, who themselves were divided in different groups: on the one hand, the brothers from the cloister of Arcella, on the other, those from Santa Maria. Each group laid total claim to the Saint. They pressed real or imagined reasons to justify their claim. They invented clever maneuvers and sought the protection of the powerful; they even resorted to force and to arms, thus running the risk of civil war. The sisters, thinking that they would succeed in keeping the body for themselves, played all the cards, from clever maneuvers to streams of unconsolable tears. On the one hand, they begged with tears that they be allowed to keep the body of the master whom they had honored and loved. On the other hand, they courted the powerful people in the city to win their agreement. Since they lived under the rules of a strict cloister, they could not do this personally. Therefore, they made use of the monks from Arcella as the messengers of their wishes. And the monks had the same interests.

'The rulers of the city, the members of the Order, and the noble laity' could not simply ignore these demands since the Poor Clares themselves came from highly placed families. Besides, people in positions of power have no desire to create enemies or to disturb the peace unnecessarily. Thus, they promised their support. But in the end, the 'poor Ladies' discovered that it was all only a 'sailor's yarn' and that the clever politicians had access to many back doors. We must recall that, at that time, the city was divided into four sections. Broadly speaking, these correspond to the four directions of the heavens. To the north, there was Capo di Ponte, which included Arcella; to the south, Torricelli; to the east, Altinate; and to the west, the cathedral area. The rivalries broke out immediately, and the people of Capo di Ponte came to press their claims at the cloister. They said: he who has died here should remain here. In order to make their intentions clear, they showed their weapons and posted an armed guard at the cell.

Some days after this, the monks from Santa Maria arrived on the scene. They wanted to take the corpse with them, to celebrate the burial in their church — which had also been his church — and give Anthony a worthy burial place. Beside this, they had two other reasons for their plan: Anthony had had a special love for this place where he had spent considerable time, and when his death was near, he had expressed the desire to return there. There was no doubt about his final intention. And there was no reason for not respecting his last wish. But with the instigation of the monks and Poor Clares of Arcella, no one at Capo di Ponte was interested in listening to reason. The poor monks who had come out from the city found themselves confronted with weapons and had to turn back without achieving their purpose.

They appealed immediately to the bishop. Jacobo Corrado listened to them, called his canonists and the friars of the two fighting factions together, and had the arguments presented again. He was already aware of them; but, circumspect and well-informed as he was, he wanted to have them stated in public in the hope that the fury might abate and the voice of reason might emerge. In the end, he decided in favor of transferring the body, but turned to the mayor, Badoer, who was responsible for the public order. He did not ask him for help; rather 'he gave him the task' of looking after peace and order as the naive chronicler puts it. The answer from Capo di Ponte came quickly. In a meeting, the elders decided to resist to the utmost, and they swore an oath to place their lives and their possessions on the line in the pursuit of their goal. At first, they thought of stealing the corpse in order to get it out from under the control of their opponents. But in the end, they gave up this plan in favor of a suggestion which had been accepted also by their opponents: to await the arrival of the minister provincial. Both parties hoped to gain support from this visit. In the meantime, because of the heat and its effect on the body of the deceased, it was decided to place the corpse in a wooden coffin and to bury it temporarily nearby.

But this well-advised concern quickly led to a genuine

plot. The disappearance of the body ignited the anger of the opposition, who stormed the convent and could not be pacified until the 'precious treasure' had been dug up and found again. Fortunately, just as these events were coming to a climax, the long-awaited provincial arrived. It was on a Saturday evening. The people of Capo di Ponte placed their arguments before the assembly which was called together immediately. They strengthened their position by making open threats. The provincial, Albert of Pisa, was more clever than they. He wanted time to make his decision, and held the people there by entrusting them the flattering task of guarding the burial-place and the corpse of the Saint.

Convinced that he could not solve the problem alone, the provincial left Arcella to seek advice as to how to deal with so many actions and counter-actions. The next day he went to the mayor at the town hall to ask his advice and to obtain his help. However, even though the mayor was known to be decisive and energetic, he did not want to take any risks in the affair. In the final analysis, the burial of a friar minor did not fall under his competence. After he had heard the city council, Mayor Badoer passed the "hot potato" on to the bishop. But he decided that in the future, the grave would be guarded by city guards rather than by one of the fighting parties. And he forbade anyone to come to Arcella with weapons.

On the following Monday during the assembly of the clergy, Bishop Corrado could notice that the "underground activity" of the Poor Clares had borne some fruit, since quite a few of the clergy were in favor of Arcella. The minister provincial of the friars stood up and spoke firmly for the view that the body of Anthony ought to be brought to Santa Maria for reasons that were well known. To those who did not want to respect the last wish of the deceased he answered that the monks were bound to the orders of their superiors by virtue of the vow of obedience! Naturally the bishop saw this as a way out. It removed from him the responsibility and the risk of a decision. He decided, therefore, that the official orders of the provincial were to be observed. He charged the clergy to attend the celebration of the burial on the next day, and again he gave the mayor the 'commission' to take action against anyone who disturbed the peaceful order of the celebration. With that, he closed the meeting.

To trust is good; not to trust is better. So thought Badoer, and he arranged that the procession would not pass over the Ponte Molino. Therefore, in the early morning hours, he saw to it that a bridge of boats was built in the eastern part of the city. To the people of Capo di Ponte this appeared as yet another challenge, and they destroyed it in a few minutes. But with this, they had gone too far. The city took action against this provocation and was ready to send in its troops. The most fanatic people really expected nothing else. But some among the friars and nuns of Arcella, began to have pangs of conscience as they sensed the problem. They feared that there would be a reckoning to pay for the tragic events that began to unfold. So they urged that the body of the Saint be brought forth as quickly as possible.

This was an unconditional capitulation which made them look ridiculous, but the mayor had a special way of handling the more incorrigible fanatics. He caught them with a clever trick and brought them to the southern section of the city, where he kept them for an entire day. Anyone who would attempt to flee was threatened with the loss of their property. Only in this way was it possible for the procession to make its way forward, to pass over the Ponte Molino (from whose tower Galileo Galilei would later study the heavens), and move across the city to Santa Maria. Here the bishop celebrated the funeral service, blessed the corpse, and laid it in a marble sarcophagus which belonged to the cathedral. The day ended with this beautiful gesture. It was Tuesday, June 17, 1231."

So runs the account of P. Scandaletti. We should not

simply shake our heads in disbelief. For all the strangeness of these events which brought Padua to the brink of a civil war, the fact remains: the possibility that matters could go this far is grounded in the fact that Anthony was held in such high regard that such means seemed appropriate for the sake of keeping his relics as close to oneself as possible. The Middle Ages did not experience the saints from the distance but from close-range. Since one expected protection from the saints, one was ready to use any means to keep them close at hand.

VIII.
THE SAINT LIVES ON

The person and work of St. Anthony can be described with the word "unusual" with many shades of meaning. There is the fact of his exceptional way of life with its uninterrupted and successful work. Then, there were the turbulent events that took place between his death and his burial. But truly "unusual" is the impact he had after his death. All those who have received the gift of eternal life in Christ, but particulary the saints, do not cease to be in death. They live on, and in those who venerate them, they show that they have a rich life after death. And the way in which they live on often seems to have little relation to their earthly life.

The Canonization

Certainly the canonization of Anthony was unusual.At the time when he lived and died, it was no longer adequate simply to be placed on the list of saints by a bishop in order for a person to be venerated as a saint. Naturally this happened only in those cases where there was sufficient veneration on the part of the faithful. The proof of a broad, living veneration even today is an essential presupposition for a canonization.

At the time of St. Anthony, the popes had already reserved the process of canonization to themselves. Already at that time, a canonical process was required in which the life, heroic virtue, and miracles of the person to be canonized had to be examined. Even though this process was not as complicated and drawn out then as it is today, still there was always a period of time between death and canonization.

What was unusual in the case of Anthony was the fact that less than a complete year intervened between his death and his canonization. He died on June 13, 1231, and was canonized on May 30, 1232. The time was longer in the case of St. Francis. It was Gregory IX, the Pope who — as Cardinal Hugolino — had been so helpful to Francis, and who as pope had stood behind the Franciscan Order with so much help and care, who now elevated Anthony to the honors of the altar in the cathedral of Spoleto. He had known Anthony pesonally and placed his entire authority behind the speedy completion of the canonization process of the Saint from Padua.

Anthony had not yet been dead for a month when a meeting took place at Padua, wherein it was decided to approach the pope about speeding up the process of canonization. In attendance were priests, members of the city council, and citizens of Padua. They selected a delegation of people whom they sent to the pope who received them in a friendly way. But there was opposition from some of the cardinals who thought things were moving too quickly.The opposition was first of all directed to the process which was expected to take place according to canonical norms. In accordance with these norms, the pope established a local commission which was to study the conditions for canonization. This commission included the following: Jacopo Corrado, the bishop of Padua, the prior of the Dominicans, the abbot of the Benedictines, Jordan Forzate, and John of Vicenza. The last two were themselves later declared blessed.

After the commission had ended its work, a delegation of nine citizens of Padua delivered to the pope the commission's report together with the examination of witnesses and the reports of miracles. At the same time, they handed over the official appeals of the city officials and the university professors. The final phase of the process in Rome was entrusted to the bishop of Sabina. The chair-person of the group responsible for the proceedings was Cardinal John of Abbeville, formerly a Benedictine monk of Cluny.

But one of the cardinals raised the objection that, in his opinion, the entire procedure had gone too quickly. Naturally the people of Padua were sad and disappointed when this delay became known. How could one change the mind of the cardinal who objected, especially since he believed that he had to follow his conscience? Here only Anthony himself could be of assistance. And he acted in his own way. He appeared in a vision to the cardinal, helped him to change his mind, and in fact converted him into a convinced advocate. When this became known to the college of cardinals, the princes of the church would allow no further delay.

On May 30, 1232, the Feast of Pentecost, the canonization took place in the cathedral of Spoleto. Anthony was raised to the honors of the altar. With this, a fact became clear which remains clear to this day: "The miracles resound throughout the world; and your glory is imperishable" (hymn for Vespers for the Feast of St. Anthony in the Franciscan propers for the breviary). For on the occasion of the canonization, fifty-three miracles were publicized. Anthony had begun to manifest himself as the great wonder-worker in all forms of need.

After the solemn proclamation and the Te Deum, Pope Gregory IX intoned the antiphon "O Doctor Optime — O Excellent Doctor" in honor of the newly proclaimed Saint, an antiphon normally reserved for doctors of the church. It was an anticipation of the elevation of the Saint to the rank of doctor of the church which took place only in our own century. The pope set the feast of St. Anthony on June 13.

On May 31, 1232, the pope sent a message "to our

beloved sons, the rulers and the people of Padua," in which he officially announced the canonization to the city. On June 23, 1232, this event was announced to the universal church by a papal bull, which as usual, contained a review of the process that had just been closed and stated about Anthony: Therefore, "he has deserved not to be hidden under a basket, but to be placed on one of the undying lamp-stands of the Catholic church."

The Memorial Church at Padua

After the canonization, the influential people of Padua thought immediately about setting up a worthy monument to Anthony in the form of a church building. Naturally, the friars were also enthusiastic about the plan. In thinking of this building, they had an eye on the stream of pilgrims that had already begun to come. But the city as well was interested in adding to its fame by building a beautiful church. What tiny Assisi had done in honor of St. Francis Padua must also be able to do in honor of its Saint.

Although the work, already begun in 1232, at first on the facade, had not yet been completed, the church was recognized as a glorious structure already in 1240. At that point, the construction work was interrupted. The notorious Ezzelino had been given authority over Padua by the emperor, Frederick II. Only if he had undergone a fundamental conversion would Ezzelino have been able to encouarge or even to permit the continuation of the construction of a church in honor of Anthony of Padua who had suffered such a failure at the tyrant's hands.

Only when the tyranny had come to an end in 1256 was it possible to proceed with the work. Pope Alexander IV contributed enthusiastically to the completion of the church. He granted an indulgence of forty days to anyone who gave monetary support to its construction. This pope also set a specific dead-line: the burial-church should be completed in six years. The deadline was met. Hence, on

April 8, 1263, Anthony was solemnly transferred from the church of Santa Maria Mater Domini to the new basilica nearby. St. Bonaventure, the minister general of the Order at that time, was present for this celebration.

When the mortal remains of the Saint were examined, the miraculous fact was revealed that his tongue was incorrupt and as fresh as in life. This was rightly recognized as a sign that God wished to give honor to one who had preached and defended the Gospel of Jesus with his tongue. The tongue is preserved in a special reliquary in the basilica of St. Athony. This miraculous act of God is recalled even today in the Franciscan propers for Masses on feasts of the Order. On the feast of St. Anthony, the introduction to the Gospel is: "The tongue of the righteous is choice silver; the lips of the righteous feed many" (Prov 10:20a, 21a).

The identity of the architect of this first church in honor of Anthony is unknown. It is hardly correct to surmise that it was Br. Elias, who had led the construction of the burial church of St Francis at Assisi.

Whether the church was not solid enough in its construction, or whether it was unsatisfactory for some reason, or whether it simply was not large enough, the fact is that only two years later, the city began a reconstruction of the basilica. Two workmen from the guild of architects were appointed to work with the two friars whom the Order had entrusted with the oversight of the work. This points to the possibility that the construction of the first building might not have been completely satisfactory. The new church with its main building was completed near the end of the century. Later centuries added to the basilica in accordance with their own tendencies and in line with the dominant styles, thus bringing about many changes of very diverse artistic quality.

Many of these architectural measures and even some of the changes in the artistic decorations were necessary since the basilica was damaged frequently in the course of time: storms, war, fire, and the explosion of a nearby gunpowder factory (in the year 1617). At the beginning of the sixteenth century, work was begun on the construction of a new burial chapel to which the remains of the Saint were transferred. This addition still stands today. It may be less well-known that in the terms of the Lateran Treaty between the Italian state and the Vatican in the year 1929, the basilica and the convent of San Antonio became the property of the Vatican. A papal delegate commissioned by the pope safeguards the rights of the apostolic see.

The Relics

As we have already said, in 1263 when the relics of the Saint were transferred to the church built for that purpose, it was discovered that the tongue was preserved intact. The bones were placed in a sarcophagus which rested on four marble pillars in the middle of the church. People who wanted to pray to the Saint for his intercession would crawl into the open space under the sarcophagus.

In the year 1350, another arrangement of the relics was undertaken. Among other details, the chin was placed in its own reliquary; the other bones and the tunic were divided into three groups, each wrapped in cloth and laid in a small coffin and then placed in the marble sarcophagus. At this time, the sarcophagus with the relics was moved to a side chapel on the left side of the church where they remain to the present time. There is a valuable relic of Anthony in the Franciscan friary of St. Anna in Munich. It is the lower piece of the upper right arm. At the beginning of the fourteenth century, the minister general, Michael of Cesena, had given this relic to the emperor, Ludwig the Bavarian.

On January 6, 1981, when the relics of Anthony were removed from the sarcophagus and carefully examined, it was discovered that the coffin mentioned above was wrapped in a large yellow cloth. In the coffin there were three wrapped packets containing the mortal remains of the Saint: the bones and the skull, together with hair and small pieces of bones and the habit.

A number of interesting conclusions about Anthony were drawn from the medical examination. He was about 1.68 meters tall, therefore somewhat taller than the average man of that time. The skull is oval and elongated. Insofar as can be determined from the facial bones, his face was of a noble form. The nose is aquiline in form. In general, Anthony had the characteristics common to the Atlantic-Mediterranean race. On the leg bones below the knee there is a clear protrusion, likely the result of kneeling frequently in prayer on stone surfaces. This confirms the claim of the oldest biographies that Anthony had spent many hours of the day and night in meditation and prayer. The bones of the legs are thickly developed. With this, there is anatomical confirmation of the fact that the Saint had undertaken numerous journeys on foot through diverse countries.

Furthermore, the remains of the tongue were found with a wide layer of skin from the lower portion of the chin. With this the two pyramid-shaped cartilaginous pieces of the larynx which control the movement of the vocal cords were found to be perfectly preserved. Apparently God wished not only the tongue (the Latin word "lingua" means "tongue" but also "language") but the entire voice mechanism to remain intact. For it was with this the Saint had so powerfully defended the faith and the poor. The general condition of the relics does not allow for any decision about the illness that might have caused his death.

The Veneration of the Great Miracle Worker

Naturally the world-wide veneration of St. Anthony spread out from his burial place. Already five years after his death, in the year 1236, measures taken by the city officials indicate that it was necessary to deal with a great stream of pilgrims. As on the feasts of the Mother of God and the Apostles, so on the feastdays of St. Anthony the shops were not open for business. Merchants who did not observe this were punished with a fine of twenty soldi. The only exception to this was for those shops that sold food for the people of the town. Candles which were at times of great size were offered at the grave of the Saint. Processions took place. Sick people of all sorts were brought to his relics. At first, when the sarcophagus with the relics was elevated on the four pillars leaving a free space below, the sick were simply placed in this area directly below the relics.

As was the case with many saints, the celebration of the feast of St. Anthony was not limited to the church. It soon developed into a folk-festival with an annual fair. This fair, which is still customary in Padua on the feast of St. Anthony, began eight days before the feast itself and lasted during the entire octave. Soon the city administration saw the necessity of taking certain precautions for the feast in order to avoid chaos. The mayor had to appoint soldiers with banners and weapons as guards. Players, procurers, and prostitutes were required to remain out of the plaza in front of the church under a penalty of ten pounds. Twenty guards, four town-criers, and one notary had to be present day and night.

Finder of Lost Things

Saints venerated by the people are patrons each in his or her own area of responsibility. But Anthony is seen to be responsible for practically any sort of need by those who venerate him. In popular piety, he is appealed to most emphatically as the one who recovers lost objects. This particular responsibility goes back to the thirteenth century. It is not known how this came about. Some role may have been played by the hymn which says that he can restore "lost property and limbs." The mention of "lost limbs" likely refers to the young man who, in extreme remorse, cut off his foot only to have it restored by Anthony. But why does Anthony restore lost objects? A Doctor of the Church who concerns himself with the disorderly and the forgetful!

In his work and preaching, Anthony was very strongly orientated to practise. He knew that theology could be and had to be translated "into life." And this characteristic marks his influence after his death as well. As the "finder of lost things," Anthony proves himself to be a theologian who possesses the famous "Sitz im Leben." When a person mislays or loses something, he or she is inclined to blame the entire world, to become unloving, and to react in a nervous way. But the person who turns to Anthony experiences the fact that he or she is praying instead of complaining. And when such a person promises the Saint to give something to the poor, that person is turned in love to his or her neighbor instead of being suspicious and lacking in love. Is this not a question of relevant theology related to life, which in practical life transforms things for the good? "Teacher of the Gospel" as Doctor of the Church; and "Finder of Lost Things." In Anthony of Padua it is easy to recognize the relation between these two titles which seem so fundamentally different.

St. Anthony's Bread

In many churches there is a poor-box with the inscription: St. Anthony's Bread. Or at least, this was the case until the iconoclasm of one-sided and therefore falsely understood liturgical renovation of many churches did away with many elements of popular piety. It should be well-known to all that an offering for the poor was intended with this. How did this custom come into existence? By way of exception, the beginning of this custom can be dated exactly. On August 12, 1890, Louise Bouffier of Toulon, France, tried without success to open the lock on her door. Even a locksmith who was called in to help was unsuccessful despite his skill. He went away to get a tool to break the door open. Miss Bouffier would have felt bad if the forced opening had done damage to the door. So she made a promise to St. Anthony that she would give bread to the poor if the door was not damaged. The locksmith returned, and just to be sure, he tried it with the key once more. And the door opened with no resistance.

As a sign of her gratitude, Louise Bouffier placed a statue of St. Anthony in her shop together with a poor-box. The idea caught on. While at the beginning, only a few people came to the shop with petitions for Anthony, the number gradually increased. After a time, letters with petitions from many people were sent to Anthony in the shop. Money-offerings were sent with the understanding that they would be used to buy bread for the poor. In the year 1892, exactly two years after the affair with the locked door that initiated the practise, 5,443 francs were contributed. In the next year contributions amounted to 38,481 francs, and in 1894 the total had risen to 108,506 francs that came only to the shop in Toulon. About 2,000 letters a month came to St. Anthony in the shop.

The example was taken up in many other places; for example, by the Augustinians in Bordeaux, who took in 70,000 francs as St. Anthony's Bread for the poor already in 1894. Eventually, there was hardly a church in which one would not find a statue or a picture of the Saint with a poor-box for "St. Anthony's Bread."

Here again the practical theology of St. Anthony manifested itself. He brought it about that people did not remain closed up in their own need, but would open themselves in love to help the poor.

It would take us far afield to list the many areas in which people have turned to Anthony for help. Certainly superstition has been mixed with the veneration of Anthony. But, who is to be the judge when we are dealing with simple, straight-forward human beings who are in need? They turn to the Saint with great trust. Whatever the case may be, he brings them to prayer and to love, and thus frequently brings about the transformation of the petitioner.

Part 2
"Doctor of
the Gospel"

When Pope Gregory IX canonized Anthony on May 30, 1232, he spontaneously intoned the antiphon: "O Doctor optime — O Excellent Doctor." This antiphonal praise is normally reserved for Doctors of the Church. In this way, the pope wished to honor a saint whom he had already, during the Saint's life, described as a "Ark of the (New) Testament."

On January 16, 1964, Pope Pius XII "ratified" what Pope Gregory IX had anticipated by raising Anthony to the dignity of doctor of the church. In the tradition of the church, the doctors of the church had a title which characterizes their life, and above all, their teaching. Anthony received the title "Doctor evangelicus — Doctor of the Gospel." This was done by a papal encyclical. Such papal documents are characterized by the fact that already in their first words they announce the main theme of the document. The letter of Pius XII begins with the words: "Exulta Lusitania felix — Rejoice, Happy Portugal." This is almost a form of reparation for Portugal. For Anthony, indeed, came from Portugal, even though he was and is still commonly called the Saint of Padua.

I.
THE SERMONS

Anthony had been commissioned by Francis to educate the brothers in theology so that they would be more capable of meeting the demands of the proclamation of the Gospel in their sermons. The presentation of the life and work of the Saint has indicated clearly what sort of difficulties were involved for the preaching of the Christian faith at that time.

Certainly Anthony fulfilled his task by means of lectures. But his confreres pressured him to give them assistance of a more enduring nature. Hence, in his later years, he set about working out two cycles of sermons: the so-called "Sermones dominicales" (Sermons for Sundays of the Church Year) and the so-called "Sermones festivi" (Sermons for Feast Days during the Church Year).

The first cycle was worked out fully. But it contains not only Sunday sermons. Following the twelfth Sunday after Pentecost, there are four "Sermones in festivitatibus beatae Mariae Virginis — Sermons for the Feasts of the Blessed Virgin Mary." These include the feasts of the Nativity of Mary, the Annunciation, the Purification, and the Assumption of Mary into Heaven.

Anthony was unable to complete the second cycle with the feast-day sermons. He had interrupted work on this during the Lenten period of the year 1231; he could not have known that his imminent death would make it impossible for him to complete this work. He had gotten as far as the memorial of St. Paul. According to the liturgical calendar of that time, this would have been July 30.

In the prologue of his work, Anthony himself explains how he came to work on this collection of sermons. The instigation was the "requests and the love of the brothers, who have pressed me to this work." As a famous preacher, Anthony was asked by his confreres to give some help for their work out of his own experience. Thus, he created a work that could serve for the remote and for the immediate preparation of sermons.

But this is not a question of written sermons that were actually given in this form. It is far more a question of outlines of sermons which could provide the preacher with a plan and with some material. This becomes clear in the introductions to many of the sermons, which contain warnings and suggestions that are aimed directly at the preacher himself.

Basically, these were not fully developed sermons such as we find in many sermon books today. Many modern collections offer sermons which ought to be or at least could be given just as they are presented. Anthony himself never uses the concept of "sermon" to describe this collection of material. He speaks either of his "opus = work" or more expressly of the "work of the Gospels." From a literary point of view, Anthony presents tracts which provide the preacher with a wealth of material for the individual days. The range of the tracts varies. Most of the Sunday sermons contain as many as five "partial sermons." Also the feast-day sermons contain two or three. "Partial sermons" of an allegorical or moral character are added to these.

Now, instead of saying anything more about the style of Anthony's sermons, it seems better to look at what Anthony himself has to say about the matter. In the prologue to the Sunday sermons, he speaks of the style of his work. We will follow the comments of the Saint himself, making use of the translation of Willi Egger:

" 'Purest gold,' as is said in the first book of Paralipome-
non (I Chron), 'was the material which David gave for the
construction of a wagon for the throne of the cherubim
who surmounted the Ark of the Lord with outspread
wings.'

It is written in the book of Genesis: The gold comes
from the land of Havilath, and the gold of that land is
exceptionally good. Havilath means 'to give birth' and
signifies Sacred Scripture which is the land that first gives
birth to the shoot, then to the ear of corn, and then to the
kernels on the ear. The shoot stands for allegory, which
builds up faith, . . . the ear (which comes from spica,
spiculum = spear) stands for morality, which forms action
and penetrates the soul with its sweetness; the mature
kernel stands for anagogy, which deals with the fullness of
angelic joy and happiness. The best gold comes from the
land of Havilath, since holy understanding is drawn from
the text of Sacred Scripture. As gold surpasses all other
metals, thus the (holy) understanding surpasses all the
other sciences. A person who is not familiar with sacred
science does not understand the other sciences. Therefore
it says that David gave the purest gold.

David means merciful, or strong with his hands, or
worthy of seeing, and signifies the Son of God who was
merciful in the incarnation, strong in suffering, and worthy of seeing in eternal happiness . . . Therefore, our David,
the Son of God, . . . gave gold, that is, the understanding
of Sacred Scripture: It is written that He opened their minds
so that they could understand Scripture; purest gold, that
is, gold that has been purged of all the dregs and all the
dross of the evil of heresy.

It is then said: so that the wagon for the throne of the
cherubim might be made therefrom. This can be translated
as the fullness of wisdom. It points to the Old and the New
Testaments, in which the fullness of knowledge is found.
This alone makes knowledge possible and makes a person

into one who knows . . .

It is for the glory of God, the edification of the soul, and the consolation of anyone who reads or hears that we have built a wagon for the throne on the foundation of both Testaments, so that the soul may be lifted up from earthly things with Elias, and may be led to the heavens and to heavenly concerns. And note that, just as a wagon has four wheels, four matters are dealt with in this work: the Sunday Gospels, the accounts of the Old Testament as they are read in the church, the introit, and the epistles of the Sunday Mass. All glory, praise, and honor be to the Son of God, therefore, the source of all things, from whom alone we look forward to the reward for this work . . . He is God, praised, glorious, and blessed for all eternity. Let the entire church say: Amen. Alleluja."

This sort of text reveals clearly the style which Anthony employs for the clarification of Scripture in his sermon outlines. To start with, he chooses a text of Scripture. He then picks out the most important words. These he explains one after the other by appealing to other texts of Scripture. In this case, the most important words are: "gold," "David," "a wagon for the throne." From these words, a series of connections with other Scriptural texts is established, employing etymologies and patristic citations. These are so numerous that it has not been possible to give all of them here in print.

We shall not delay any longer with these more technical matters but will now turn our attention directly to the content of St. Anthony's sermons so that we might see at least some points of his spirituality.

II.
ST. ANTHONY'S THEOLOGICAL STYLE

The world of Anthony's theological thought has not yet been adequately researched. He did not make things easy for later scientific study. For he did not leave any sort of systematic theological works such as a "Summa theologia" as did Thomas of Aquinas, Bonaventure, or John Duns Scotus. What remains for us are the two series of sermons which he wrote as a sort of concrete, practical introduction to homiletics. The work demanded of him by the church as a preacher left him no time for theoretical theology. What we find in the sermon-outlines is applied theology which is translated into practise. In order to arrive at a sense of a general, theoretical, theological vision, we must probe for the basis of this practical theology.

Without giving a broader description of St. Anthony's theology, it can be said that Anthony had an exceptional affinity for ascetical-mystical theology. J Heerinckx has established the fact that "the sermons of St. Anthony contain a systematic teaching with respect to mysticism and present it in a clear manner." The learned abbot, Thomas of Vercelli, a friend of Anthony, appeals to his good relation with the Saint when he points him out as a good example of how quickly someone can appropriate the teaching of the saints: Anthony "has appropriated mystical theology in such a short time that, burning with heavenly fire, he also radiated knowledge of spiritual things outward."

The mystical teaching of St. Anthony can be described as follows: It is western, that is, it does not depend on Pseudo-Dionysius, but follows Augustine, Gregory the Great, and Bernard of Clairvaux. The direction of Pseudo-Dionysius, which was deeply neo-Platonic in tone, had a strong influence on the Victorines, Hugh and Richard of St. Victor. This influence was not all for the good; for example, such matters as its doctrine of the divinization of the soul, of the divine darkness, and the suffering of God, as well as its esteem for corporal visions and revelations. The teaching of St. Anthony is free of all these elements, and is therefore purely religious.

It can also be said that the mystical doctrine of St. Anthony has a Franciscan character insofar as it is affective and practical. It is concerned with the interior love for the humanity of Christ and his suffering, and emphasizes poverty, solitude and contemplation, together with the cultivation of the ordinary virtues. Because of this basic Franciscan orientation, his doctrine is clear in its understanding of the essential issues, and can be carried out in life. Anthony does not concern himself with speculative mysticism since Scholastic speculation has had no impact on his mysticism.

Finally, his teaching is typical of Anthony himself. By this we mean that the basic source of his teaching is his own experience. His personal experience confirmed many of the teachings of his masters and opened new insights for him. But he does not confine himself almost exclusively with the description of his own mystical experiences, as is the case with Theresa of Avila, Angela of Foligno, and many other mystics.

With Anthony, we notice that he gives no description of his own spiritual experiences. He himself offers the following fundamental law of the spiritual life: "The mystery of the heart is a curtain which ought to hang between ourselves and our neighbor and which ought to keep our neighbor from looking behind this curtain. It should be sufficient for him to see the lamps held out in our hand and to be illuminated by them. Jesus alone is our high priest. All hearts stand open before him. He sees over and through the curtain, for he penetrates the heart and its secret thoughts."

What Anthony says here coincides fully with what the founder of his Order, Francis of Assisi, says so clearly in his twenty-third Admonition: "Blessed is that servant who "lays up as a treasure in heaven" (Mt 6:20) the good things the Lord has revealed to him, and who has no desire to reveal it to others with the hope of receiving a reward. For the Most High will reveal his works to whomever he will. Blessed is that servant who preserves the mysteries of the Lord in his heart (cfr. Lk 2:29.51)."

Like Francis, Anthony would like to say: In the life of a person whose heart has been grasped by the Lord there are happenings and processes that are rooted in the uniqueness of each individual person and in the personal world of each. It is there that these realities have their home and their meaning. Since these realities are so deeply grounded in the person, they ought to remain normally within the realm of that which constitutes the secret of the person. It is not appropriate to make such things public since they then would lose their personal quality. The publication of such experiences which take place in the depths of the person — Anthony speaks of the "mystery of the heart" — is both possible and necessary insofar as this experience ought to have an impact on the person's life. Anthony speaks of this when he says that our fellow human beings ought to be satisfied to see the lamps of our readiness carried in our hands. This expression of our inner experience in the form of action is valid. The mere verbal expression can be an unproven claim.

III.
THE SON IS THE FACE
OF THE FATHER

The incarnation of the Son of God is the central mystery of the Christian faith. Yet, in view of the fact that Jesus Christ is truly God and truly human, it is difficult for theology as well as for the practise of faith to maintain the proper balance when one desires to go beyond the simple expression of this dogma of faith.

When we review the history of Christology, it is easy to show that there are always times when either the divinity of Jesus Christ is emphasized in such a one-sided way that his humanity is not taken seriously in its full measure, or **vice versa**, the humanity of Jesus Christ is so strongly emphasized that no real room remains for his divinity.

What is the situation with Anthony of Padua? His Christological statements are found not in the technical expressions of theology but in a language that translates his thought into a practical expression for the life of faith. This lends his teaching a particular validity. Not every theologian understands how to translate his thoughts into practical terms in a way that is clearly understandable.

For Anthony's Christology, a decisive point of departure seems to lie in the conversation between Jesus and his disciples where the disciples asked him: "We do not know where you are going: how can we know the way?" The Lord answered: "I am the way, and the truth, and the life. No one comes to the Father, but by me. If you had known me, you would have known my Father also. Henceforth you know him and have seen him." But the Apostles did not understand what these words were supposed to reveal to them. Therefore they asked through Philip: "Lord, show us the Father, and we shall be satisfied." By asking for the ability to see the Father, they were asking that the deepest mystery of Christ be revealed to them. To this lack of understanding Christ answered clearly: "He who has seen me has seen the Father. Believe me that I am in the Father and the Father in me" (Jn 14:6-11).

For Anthony, this self-revelation of the Lord stands as the guiding idea for everything that he thinks or says about Christ. Thus, he remains close to the words of Christ in his explanation: "If you know me, you know my Father also. From now on, recognize him, for you have seen him. It is as though he is speaking about two equal persons when he says: If you have seen this one, you have seen the other. For they had seen the Son who is fully equal. But he warns them that they ought to think of the Father in this way and in no other way: In me, whom you know, you have already seen him. For I am like him in all things, and you have seen me."

In another place, Anthony is as brief as he is deep when he says: "The Son is the face of the Father. As we recognize someone by his face, so we recognize the Father through the Son."

From the time of the conception and birth of Christ onward, God no longer speaks to humanity as he had in the Old Testament: "You cannot see me" (Ex 33:20). Instead of this, now a human being stands on this earth and says: "He who sees me, sees the Father also." The one whom the Scriptures describe as "dwelling in inaccessible light" (1 Tim 6:16) has allowed himself to be seen and touched in Jesus Christ. Anthony emphasizes this over and over:

"As the beam of light comes down from the sun and sheds light on the world, and yet is not separated from the sun, so also the Son of God has come out from the Father, and has enlightened the world, and yet has not been separated from his Father. Indeed, he is one with his Father, as he himself says: "I and the Father are one" (Jn 10:30).

"The Son is the face of the Father. As we recognize someone by his face, so we recognize the Father through the Son. The light of the face (Ps 4:7) of God is the knowledge of the Son and the enlightenment through faith."

Anthony is of the opinion that in the incarnation of his Son, God does not enter a territory that is totally foreign to him or totally unrelated to himself. For Holy Scripture says that humanity was created in the image of God and that everything was created through the eternal Word of God. The incarnation of Christ is not a fully new beginning with no presuppositions. Rather, in dealing with humanity, God enters into relationship with a being that, already by virtue of creation, is an image of God and carries the impression of the eternal Word of the Father. God enters into the realm of his image, to that level of reality that already bears the stamp of God.

Anthony develops this insight thoroughly. He takes seriously the word of Scripture: "God created man in His own image, in the image of God He created him" (Gen 1:27). Building on this statement, he says: "God created man from the earth, and created him in His own image so that he might exist, live, feel, and have memory, reason and will." In this way it becomes clear that Anthony wishes to acknowledge a trinitarian character in humanity. He developed this further with the following words: "As the Son proceeds from the Father, and the Holy Spirit from both, so the will proceeds from reason, and both from memory. Without these three faculties, the soul would be incomplete, and none of these three faculties can be complete in itself."

With this, Anthony intends to say: Just as we, through

faith, know and confess that the perfection of God consists in the unity of the trinity, so humanity, as the image of God, possesses a wonderful unity of reason, will, and memory.

Anthony develops this further by appealing to the Athanasian Creed: "As 'the Father is God, the son is God and the Holy Spirit is God, and yet there are not three gods, but only one God' in three persons, so also reason is the soul, the will is the soul, and memory is the soul; and yet they are not three souls, but only one soul with three faculties. In this way, the soul is marked as the image of God in a marvelous way."

From the perspective of the God-likeness of humanity, Anthony understands the significance of the commands and admonitions which God has given to humanity. The real reason for these commands and admonitions is not to be seen in the sin and failure of humanity, although this has something to do with the question. Rather, the basis for the commands is to be seen in the fact that humanity is created in the image of God. Anthony writes that the commands are an invitation of God to humanity, an invitation to oneness of will.

In the commandments God reveals where he — God — says Yes or No. He reveals his nature. Through this revelation, God invites humanity as his image, to enter into the rhythm of God's Yes and No. Anthony has put this in picturesque language: "With the coin that bears the image and inscription of the king, that is, with the observance of the divine commands, both the clergy and the laity attain their salvation. As long as the first human being preserved this coin, he did not lose God's image and likeness."

As the commandments of God make it clear that humanity is the image of God, so Anthony understands the human conscience in the same context. In Anthony's view, conscience can be seen as the living desire of the image for God, who is the original after which the image is shaped.

Such thoughts as these allow the incarnation of the Son of God to appear in a special light. We must not overlook the fact that these thoughts about humanity have a definite historical point of departure. Anthony had been commissioned to engage in controversy with the Cathari. The dualistic theology of the Cathari manifests itself with particular clarity in their concept of the incarnation of Christ.

Briefly, according the teaching of the Cathari, the good God created the world of spiritual reality while God's adversary created the material, earthly world including human bodies. These bodies were without souls. In order to give them souls and life, the adversary won a number of souls from the good God to follow him in the created world and to unite themselves with these bodies. This union of body and soul is the essence of original sin. And this original sin is continued whenever another human being is conceived and born into the world. All sexual activity and conception of new life was seen as the extension of this original sin.

With this understanding according to which human existence was seen as the constant repetition of sin through which the soul was imprisoned in the body, it was impossible for the Cathari to have a genuine faith in the incarnation of Christ. They had to see it as unreasonable that God would assume a human body. Therefore, they interpreted the person of Jesus Christ in such a way that the eternal Word of God entered the ear of the Virgin Mary and took on an apparent body. The human life and death of the Redeemer were merely apparent and not real, since God wished to make himself understandable to humanity in this way. Hence, salvation was effected not by the death of the Savior, but through his teaching, through his word. From this perspective, we can understand the concern that stood behind the words of St. Anthony's sermons: "The creature has borne its Creator, the poor Virgin has carried the Son of God." "You are both the most exalted and the most humble! Lord of the angels, You are subject to men! The Creator of the heavens obeys a carpenter, the God of eternal glory becomes subject to a Virgin!"

Anthony depicts Christ as one who took on the weight of human existence not only in appearance but in reality: "Why should you, O Son of God, wear a penitential garment? It is not God, but sinful humanity, not the Creator but the sinner who, in justice, ought to wear this garment. This should be the garb of the sinner, not of the one who redeems from sin. Why should you wear a hair-shirt? It would be appropriate for the sinner in every way; indeed, it would be necessary for him, for God repented of having created humanity. Therefore the complaint of the Lord: With your sins you have given me something to cope with, through your offence, you have given me pain . . . (And yet:) the reflection of the eternal light is hidden beneath the penitential robe of the body."

In the Christmas liturgy, the church speaks of the "admirable commercium" — an exchange calculated to evoke wonder — which has taken place between God and humanity in the incarnation. Anthony picked up this thought and worked out many variations of it: "Christ has truly come to our aid by giving us the gift of his divinity and assuming our humanity so that we, who had been excluded, could now be taken into the Kingdom of God. He left heaven so that we might gain entrance there."

Anthony speaks of this exchange from yet another perspective: "While humanity stretched out its hand toward the glory of the heavenly majesty, God emptied himself of his own power and glory and humbly adapted himself to the poverty of human existence." "Because Adam did not wish to serve the Lord in paradise, the Lord has assumed the form of a servant in order to serve the servant, so that the servant would no longer be ashamed to serve the Lord."

And there is that very concise statement which could be taken formally as the key to the spirituality of St.

Anthony: "He came to you so that you might come to Him."

It remains to add to these Christological thoughts of St. Anthony yet another point that is not unessential. Anthony says in the form of a prayer: "You became human for us human beings, in order to redeem us. From all that you have suffered, you have learned mercy. To none of the angels can we say: Behold, you are of our flesh and bone. But to you, the Son of God, we can say in all truth that you are of our flesh and bone. For you have not assumed an angelic nature but the nature of the descendents of Abraham. Be merciful to us, therefore, since we are of your flesh and bone. For who despises his own flesh? But you are our brother and our flesh. Therefore you must have mercy and compassion for your poor brothers. For we have but one Father, you by nature and we by grace. You have power in the house of your Father. Do not exclude us from sharing in that holy inheritance, for we are your flesh and bone. In the past, the children of Israel carried the bones of Joseph from the land of Egypt to the land of promise. Lead us, who are your flesh and bone, from this Egyptian darkness into the land of the saints."

After this rather lengthy citation, we would like to make a side remark. With his extensive knowledge of the Scriptures, Anthony maintains a very close relationship with the words of Scripture when he expresses his own thoughts. He does not do this in the modern style which makes it possible to know precisely where we ought to look in the Bible to find support for our own thoughts by appealing to the word of God, and to know exactly where the quotation marks are to be placed at the beginning and end of a citation. In the text from Anthony which we have cited there are many allusions to texts of the Scriptures which would have to be traced if one were preparing a critical edition of the text today. Anthony lives and thinks so thoroughly from the word of God in the Old and the New Testaments that his presentation is enlivened throughout by the words of Scripture. He shows himself to be a "Teacher of the Gospel," the title given to him as a Doctor of the Church. This is in no way to deny that he knew and used the work of others to open up and understand the Holy Scriptures.

What becomes clear in this citation is the following: Anthony does not see the incarnation of Christ as a phase that came to an end with the resurrection and ascension, as though the human nature of Christ had a function which was carried out in his earthly life and crucifixion so that there was no further use for it. When Anthony addresses the glorified Lord with the words: "You are our flesh and bone," he expresses his conviction that, in his resurrection and ascension, Christ did not lay aside his human nature like a mantle that had fulfilled its function, but he remains human even in the glory of God. These thoughts should have great significance for a Christian spirituality, that is, for a spirituality that takes its direction from Christ. For in the center of this thought stands the human existence of Christ with all its concreteness and permanence.

As we said in the beginning, the depiction of the Child Jesus on the arm of the Saint comes relatively late. But we can well see that there is a deeper, inner justification for bringing Anthony in such an intimate relation with the incarnation of the Son of God. Certainly, Anthony is aware of the fact that we can never grasp the mysterious depths of the incarnation of Christ on this earth, and that this mystery will be opened to us only when we contemplate God in eternity.

In explaining why three Masses are celebrated on the feast of the birth of the Lord, Anthony writes: "We celebrate the first Mass at night because that birth from the Father remains mysterious even for those who believe in it. We celebrate the second Mass in the morning at daybreak, since we can know his birth from his mother, but it is hidden by a certain veil. Who can untie the thong of his sandal (Jn 1:27); who can penetrate the mystery of his incarnation? We celebrate the third Mass in bright daylight because in the day of eternity, when all darkness is over, we will clearly recognize the birth of Jesus Christ from the Father and from his mother. Then we will know him who knows all, for we will see him eye to eye, and we will be as he is (cf. 1 Jn 3:2)."

"To be as he is:" this possibility begins for us in a seminal form already on this earth. For this is the ultimate meaning of the discipleship to which Christ calls us. Anthony makes this very clear when he compares the life of Christ with the ladder which Jacob, the patriarch, had seen in a vision: "Jacob saw the ladder" (Gn 28:12) on which you can ascend to Mount Tabor. Note that this ladder has two beams and six rungs for climbing. The two beams are an image for the divinity and the humanity of Christ. The six rungs are an image of his poverty and humility, his wisdom and mercy, his patience and obedience . . . This ladder touched the earth when he preached and worked miracles, but it touched the heavens when he spent the night in prayer, as Luke reports (11:12). Behold, the ladder is set up! Why do you not wish to climb it? Why do you crawl on the earth on your hands and knees? Climb up, you angels, you prelates of the church, and all you who believe in Jesus Christ. Climb up, I say to you, and behold how good is the Lord. (Ps 33:9). Then climb down to be of help and to give advice, for your neighbor is in need of assistance! . . . Do you believe there is any other way for you to move onward to Mount Tabor — to peace in the light, and to the glory and joy of heaven — except on the ladder of humility, poverty and the suffering of Christ? Truly, there is no other way. The Lord himself has said: "If anyone would follow me, let him deny himself and take up his cross on himself and follow me (Mt 16:24)."

What Anthony says here in a rather drawn out fashion is expressed briefly in the shorter passages from his sermons: "Three kinds of seed have been sown on the earth by Christ: his holy and praiseworthy life, the proclamation of the Kingdom of Heaven, and his miracles." Christians are called to accept the life, the words, and the works of Christ with an open heart and allow these to bear fruit a hundredfold in the field of a ready and willing heart. Certainly this is the concern of Christian preaching. But the realization of it is the task of each Christian. It is a question of internalizing the life, the words, and the works of Christ so that this can bring forth fruit in human life.

IV.
IF ANYONE WISHES TO PRAY OR TO MEDITATE BETTER

In the previous chapter we have seen the central role which the incarnation — the human being of the Son of God — had for the spirituality of St. Anthony. He simply took the words of Christ seriously: "He who sees me sees the Father also." "I am the way, the truth, and the life."

This becomes clear also in the area of prayer, which is so important for Christian spirituality. Anthony explains his understanding of the relation between these in a somewhat extended statement:

"If anyone wishes to pray or to meditate better, let that person place before him or herself the humanity of Christ, his birth, his suffering, and his resurrection in clear images; for our weak spirit, which can think only in bodily terms and images, will discover an object which speaks to us and to which we can turn the eye of piety in an appropriate way. Thus, Christ appears in the form of the mediator. And when the human person, according to the word of Job (5:24), discovers the essence of the mystery of Christ, he or she will not sin. In other words, when a person turns the eyes of his or her love to Christ and contemplates him the human manifestation of the love of God, that person will never again be separated from him. And since faith sees no separation of the human from the divine in him, that person will come to recognize God in this human manifestation. This style of meditation helps the poor in spirit (Mt 5:3) and enables the simple children of God to discover greater joy in love as they draw ever closer to his humanity. But later, when faith has passed over into love, the contemplatives hold Jesus Christ at the center of their heart in a sweet embrace — totally human because of the human nature he assumed, and fully God because of the God who assumed the human nature. Then they begin to recognize Christ not only in his visible form, even though they are never able to grasp him fully in his divine nature. Then they gladly offer their gifts; for, in their hearts, they hold Christ to be holy (1 Pt 3:15).

What Anthony says here is thoroughly Christian; that is, it bears the imprint of Christ. When it is a question of developing the spiritual life in the central area of prayer, Anthony offers neither training nor particular techniques for prayer. But he singles out the most important presuppositions for prayer: quiet, recollection, self-awareness. More important for him is the content of prayer and meditation: the object, or better, the person around whom the efforts of the spiritual life revolve. For the intention of the person who prays or meditates is finally directed to that which determines the person, that which totally fills the person in meditation.

Whether I call the process of genuine prayer and meditation a passing over the other, or receiving the other into myself, the fact is that by this circling, or penetrating, or allowing myself to be filled, the object of contemplation fills the entire horizon of my life and experience in proportion to the intensity of the process so that my life moves in the rhythm of the other.

The only attitude that can make this possible is the readiness to surrender oneself, or a sense of devotion which is not filled out with any particular emotional elements and is not simply identical with particular experiences. Devotion or self-surrender is the attitude in which the I of the human person surrenders its tendency to affirm itself in the face of the Greater, and allows itself to be led and determined totally by the Greater.

This is exactly what Anthony means in the previously cited text when he speaks of the poor in spirit and the simple children of God. The issue is expressed even more deeply with the concept of the "simple" if we understand that concept in terms of the rich content which it had in the area of spirituality at the time of Anthony. In Franciscan literature there is the well-nigh classical account of the simple Br. John, a companion of St. Francis.

In his Life of Francis, Thomas of Celano says about this brother that Francis "made him his special companion because of his grace of simplicity." John was a farmer before he found Francis. He was a man who knew and accepted his limits. In view of the uncertainty that his limits imposed on him, he took the life of Francis as the measuring rod to indicate for him the proper way to act. He did this not in the sense of a "following" but in the sense of a "mimicking" of Francis down to the most meaningless details. The account of Thomas of Celano says: "He watched him as his model and copied everything he did. The saint noticed this, and asked him why he did these things. He answered: 'I have promised to do everything that you do. It would be dangerous for me to omit anything. The saint rejoiced at the brother's simplicity, but gently forbade him to act in this way in the future. Not long after this, the simple brother went to the Lord in this purity. The saint often proposed his life for imitation. And with great joy, he called him Saint John rather than Brother John."

Thomas of Celano adds a few words to this account which reveal the deeper significance of the behavior of the simple John: "Note that it is a mark of pious simplicity to live according to the counsels of those who are greater than yourself, and always to support yourself on the example and principles of the saints. O, that it were given to human wisdom to follow him reigning in heaven at least with the same zeal with which pious simplicity attempted to conform itself to him on earth."

This closing remark of the biographer points out an

essential but often overlooked concern of the spiritual life; that is, a life led by and filled by the Spirit of God. What the biographer is saying — viewed from the perspective of John, the Simple — is said with respect to Francis. For John, Francis is the greater according to whose counsel he desires to live; Francis is the saint on whose example he wishes to support himself. Viewed from the perspective of Thomas of Celano, Francis is the one who is reigning in heaven; he is the one to whom the simple Br. John wished to conform himself while on earth. And now Celano says that it would truly be a postulate of human wisdom at least now to follow the one who is glorified in heaven.

Here we clearly sense that the closing remark is very basic in nature, and moves beyond the relation between Br. John and Francis. Indeed, it points to the relation between St. Francis and Christ as well as to the relation of every Christian to Christ. Christ is the greater, according to whose counsel we are to live if we are truly simple. Christ is the saint on whose example and principles we will support ourselves if we are led by simplicity. Christ is the one who rules in heaven. We follow him, and we attempt to conform our lives to his earthly life if we are simple.

As we notice here, simplicity has nothing to do with lack of talent or deficient intelligence. Simplicity means to recognize that there is someone greater, Christ, to whom we ought to look in directing our lives. Simplicity means to recognize the example and the counsel of Christ, and simply to follow them. It means that we try not to place speculations or distorting interpretations between hearing the word of God and our attempt to live according to it; for such interpretations often amount to finding reasons for not following God's word. Simplicity means to take the short and uncomplicated route from hearing the word of God, or from the encounter with God, to action.

In discussing simplicity, Thomas of Celano points to this immediate translation of God's word into action when he speaks of the direct connection between simplicity and

wisdom. To us wisdom and simplicity seem to be irrecon-
cilable opposites. But Francis had spoken of them as realities that are closely related. In his greeting to the virtues
he says: "Hail to you, Queen Wisdom. May the Lord preserve you together with your sister, holy, pure Simplicity."

A person who listens to the word of divine wisdom
with simplicity, accepting it and following it without hesi-
tation, is led and directed by the wisdom of God. To the
degree that the simple person carries out and fulfills the
word of God, which is an encounter with the eternal God
of wisdom, that person partakes in eternal wisdom. At first
hearing, to speak of "simplicity" in the context of "spirituality" sounds unusual. Yet there is a profound relation
here. We can say: genuine spirituality means to be led by
the Spirit of God. And this is possible only on the basis of
simplicity. It is exactly this that Anthony says when he
speaks about prayer. Let us repeat it briefly: "If anyone
wishes to pray and meditate better, let that person place
before him or her the humanity of Christ, his birth, his
suffering, and his resurrection in clear images." To this he
adds: "This style of meditation helps the poor in spirit and
enables the simple children of God to discover greater joy
in love as they draw ever closer to his humanity."

Simplicity makes it possible for human beings to enter
without reservation into the mystery of salvation, namely,
the mystery of God becoming a human being. In a religious sense, simplicity means letting oneself enter totally
into the words of Christ: "'I am the way . . . No one comes
to the Father except through me (Jn 14:6).

In view of this revelation, one does not seek one's
"own" way. Without any "if" or "but," we look to Christ
and follow him by the short way which simplicity takes
from hearing to doing. This is exactly what Anthony
means when he says that we can best develop our prayer
and meditation by beginning with the way in which God
has revealed himself to humanity. This took place not in
abstract doctrines but in the concreteness of the humanity

of Jesus Christ.

It is most in harmony with the structures of the human spirit if we recall the entire event of the human mystery of Jesus Christ with our spritual imagination, for the human soul begins with the concrete, even though it moves eventually from the concrete to the abstract level of thought. Anthony expresses this clearly.

He is also of the opinion that if we give ourselves without reservation to the humanity of the Son of God, we will be led by the Son of God himself to a knowledge of God in this human form. This personal bond between the person who prays and meditates and the God-man leads us to the living center of the Christian life and to the richness of the divine life.

At this point, Anthony offers very clear advice which needs to be reflected on today when there is so much concern for methods and styles of prayer and meditation. Even though these may have some justification as preparations for meditation in the proper sense, they are not born out of the center of Christian faith. Christian prayer and meditation must lead to an encounter with a Thou, with a person, with the Thou of God in the person of Jesus Christ. Indeed, in the final analysis, the question remains whether the person at prayer is satisfied with this direct way of simplicity, or whether he or she wishes to approach God with pride in one's assumed intellectual accomplishments.

In the Middle Ages, Anthony was considered one of the great masters of the spiritual life. In addition to this very basic advice, we find in Anthony other concrete suggestions which can be helpful for the proper orientation to prayer. In one place he writes: "The correct order for our prayer and petition to God is shown to us by the Apostle (1 Tim 2:1) when he writes: 'First of all I urge you: Come to God with supplications, prayers, intercessions, and thanksgiving."

Anthony explains these four dimensions of our encounter with God in the following way: "Supplication in the spiritual life means an anxious calling to God; for God, who gives us true knowledge, before he comes to our aid with grace, sends us nothing but pain." This is the phase in which the person who turns to God can give the impression that he or she can go no farther, and that God does not react to his or her cry and does not come to help. We can name this phase in any way we want, even with the mystical term "dark night." Yet it is precisely here that assistance for the person seeking God enters into the picture with a particular depth. Before God's help can be perceived by the human person, God sends us nothing but pain as Anthony says. Certainly this pain is closely related to the type of knowledge about God which is given to the human person in this phase. This pain is not grounded solely in sins that have been committed. It is related also to the fact that the human person becomes aware of the immense gulf that separates the creature from the totally other, infinite God. Indeed, the human person seeks an encounter with God. Yet, that which the human person can bring in to the presence of God is ever so poor in significance.

Now, Anthony calls this the first phase. This is not meant to designate some sort of temporal order. For it is a phase which plays a role in the search for God over and over. The closer the human person approaches to God, the more obvious it becomes what a great distance stands between humanity and God. Therefore, it is an honest confession when great Christians, at the end of their lives, have said that they can now finally begin to respond to God, for up to now they had done little or even nothing of significance. This attitude is exemplary for others. Francis of Assisi made this confession very explicitly.

The second phase is described by Anthony in the following way: "A person truly prays when he or she clings to God in love and speaks with God in a quiet and trusting way. Prayer means that condition of the soul on the illuminative way in which the soul savors God as long as God permits it." Taken strictly, these words, express in a hidden way the advice of St. Anthony which we have already discussed about the importance of approaching God in an attitude of genuine simplicity. For to speak with God "in a quiet and trusting way" presupposes that the person in prayer is dealing with his or her genuine self and with the prayerful expressions of this self in the honest awareness of what it truly is. It presupposes further that the self remains what it is, and that the person brings his or her existence into this speech with God without falsifying or enhancing it. It is a question of the truth of one's own reality, borrowing nothing from anyone else.

As Anthony expresses it, this honesty makes possible a profound experience of God, an enjoyment of God, which grasps the entire person. Certainly, it is important to note that Anthony places this process on the illuminative way. To speak of the "illuminative way" may sound very exalted. But Anthony relates it to a very concrete reality. He writes: "First the Christian must be cleansed from sin. Then it is possible to enter on the illuminative way through the practise of good works."

In the understanding of mystical theology since the time of Pseudo-Dionysius, the "way of illumination" is the second level of the mystical journey to God through purgation and union. Anthony connects this illumination with human action and forbids any sort of flight that would involve the separation between experience and action. It follows the same direction as the view of one of the early companions of St. Francis, Br. Giles, who was an authority in the area of contemplation. At one time, Giles said: "A person possesses as much wisdom as the good that he or she does, and no more." Illumination, or being filled with divine wisdom, is intimately bound to concrete action. We ought to recall how Francis said that wisdom is made possible for a human person through simplicity. But simplicity means that knowledge is translated into action in a direct and uncomplicated way.

The third dimension of prayer Anthony calls petition: "We make intercession when we are concerned about gaining temporal things and those things that are necessary for our life. In the case of such prayer, God looks kindly on the good will of the person praying, but he grants only that which is for our best; and this God gives gladly to anyone who prays correctly. When we make requests of God, we ought not to turn to God with stubborn insistence on our own desire, but with self-sacrificing trust. For we do not know what it is we truly need in these temporal things; it is our heavenly Father who knows (Mt 6:8)."

What Anthony says here holds good for the entire realm of the Christian prayer of petition. Anthony gives it a special accent by making it clear that in the case of the prayer of petition, the most important and decisive thing is not the specific object asked for even though that object may be significant for the human person. The point of the prayer of petition is not to circumvent the will of God. As an encounter with God, the prayer of petition must be sustained by an openness to God's will. This is clearly expressed by the reference to the Lord's Prayer where the request for bread follows after the request for readiness to recognize the will of God as the decisive factor in our earthly life.

It is precisely this openness to the will of God pushing beyond the actual petition made in prayer that is crucial if human prayer is to be able to develop to the level of contemplation. Anthony does not recommend special techniques and methods as a preparation for contemplation. He does not see the contemplative experience as a privilege reserved for a particular group of people. What he sees as the decisive presupposition for the level of contemplative experience lies in an area that we might ordinarily not relate to prayer without some explanation.

He says: "You will not be able to see God if you do not

listen obediently. If you are deaf, then you will be blind as well. Listen in obedience, then, with a heart full of love. Then you will be able to see God with the eye of contemplation, for it is written (Sir 17:7): God implants his eye in his heart. God implants his eye in the human heart when the human person listens to God with his or her whole heart and when, therefore, God gives that person the light of contemplation."

Obedient listening is here seen as a power that opens the human person to the higher realities of God so that God can give his eye, his "way of seeing things," to the heart of the human person. We do not speak of reason here since it is a question of the deeper levels of life, of the heart, of that level of life where our decisions are really made.

This viewpoint is so important to the Saint that he repeats it in different words in another place: "If you cannot obey, you cannot see either. If you do not wish to hear, then you remain blind. Obey gladly, then, that you might see with your eyes in contemplation. But God gives the heart a light for the eyes when he infuses the light of contemplation in the human person who listens obediently with his or her entire heart. As long as the first human being was obedient in Paradise, God was the light for his eyes." When it is a question of the spiritual life, it is impossible to cultivate and develop one area in isolation from the other areas. And growth in an area as central as obedience to God will have an effect on all other areas.

A fourth dimension of prayer is suggested by Anthony when he says: "Finally we say thanks when we recognize and acknowledge God's gifts of grace. Gratitude is the honest and uninterrupted orientation of our good will toward God, even though at times the external expression or the interior love may not be active or perceptible."

"To say thanks" — in view of what Anthony says, we must consider the fact that "gratias agere" means not only to "say thanks" but "to carry out thanks in act." This is a question of the entire orientation of the human person to

God. It is an attitude of faith, an active response to the goodness of God. "To recognize and acknowledge God's gifts of grace" is the decisive element in thanksgiving, or "gratiarum actio," or in Greek, "eucharistia." Precisely in the case of the Greek expression of "eucharistia" we recognize that at this level of prayer, which Anthony numbers as the fourth, we stand before the central Christian act.

"To recognize and acknowlege God's gifts of grace." In a remarkable way, this leads the human person back to him or herself in this encounter with God which is of essential importance. For the recognition of the gifts of God's grace takes place not in an abstract, theoretical realm, but in the human experience of one's own reality. The person who believes recognizes the work of God in him or herself. Certainly we recognize this in others as well. But even there, it is in the form of a personal encounter. Thus, the attitude of thanksgiving demands that we recognize ourselves as well as our fellow human beings. Certainly, this recognition of the gifts of God's grace must include the acknowledgement that these gifts do indeed come from God.

Basically, we are looking at the attitude of the poor of God, which, for Anthony, is a decisive presupposition for progress in prayer and contemplation. Poverty of spirit, poverty before God, in the Franciscan understanding, does not mean that we should find nothing good in ourselves, or that we can do nothing that is good. Francis formulated it in the following way: "Blessed is that servant who attributes all things good to God, the Lord." The question is this attribution to God. And, according to what Anthony says in the context of thanksgiving, this takes place in the recognition and acknowledgement of that which God has done in human beings and through human beings. And this depends totally on the person's fundamental orientation which endures even though no visible action takes place and interior love is not discernible. Thanks is enacted fundamentally through consistent poverty of spirit, poverty before God. To these thoughts of St. Anthony concerning prayer, we add the following brief remarks: "We can pray in three ways: with the heart, with the mouth, and with the hands."

Anthony explains these three forms of prayer with the words of Scripture: "It is said concerning the first sort of prayer — the prayer of the heart — that 'A humble prayer pierces the clouds' (Sir 35:17)." Today we translate this text: "The prayer of the poor pierces the clouds." This amounts to the same thing as the translation of Anthony. The text is concerned with the humble prayer of the "Anawim Yahweh," as they are called in the Old Testament; that is, those people who are conscious of their poverty before God and place their trust not in themselves but in God alone. Such prayer, Anthony says, is an affair and an act of the heart. And since the decisive orientation of the human person to God is given there, expressing itself in wordless prayer, such prayer has value with God.

Anthony writes further: "It is said concerning the second type of prayer — prayer with mouth: 'Let my prayer come before you' (Ps 88:3)." The obvious meaning which Anthony sees in this citation from the Psalms is that prayer spoken with the mouth is not automatically genuine and efficacious. Rather, a genuinely humble prayer of the heart is necessary to make vocal prayer a genuine prayer.

And finally, Anthony says: "Concerning the third type of prayer — prayer with the hands — it is said: 'Pray without ceasing' (1 Thes 5:17). In this final sense, the person who never ceases doing good never ceases praying." However we may wish to describe and determine what the process of prayer consists of, the principal issue is that a person encounters God, recognizes the greatness of God, and draws the consequences from that in that he or she moves into the sphere of God. This should be understood to mean that a prayer which does not lead to consequences in action — to action directed toward God — is only an oral declamation. Prayer and action are not seen as two basically different realities by Anthony. Proper action is itself a form of prayer, in his view, because human action is a recognition of God and an expression of human dependence on God when a person, who is poor before God, understands his or her good works to be a gift of God through which God works in the human person. "To do the good" as a sign that God has taken possession of one's person is a form of prayer, in Anthony's view. Anthony does not mean a sort of pious preference for activism, as these words might seem to suggest. This becomes clear from numerous places in his sermons in which he emphasizes that especially the active person ought to withdraw often to silence and recollection in order to shape his or her life properly. In describing good action as prayer, he did not intend to elevate activity to a mere activism. Rather, he wished to maintain the inseparability of prayer and action.

V.
THE EXALTED DIGNITY
OF THE SINNER
WHO REPENTS

"He — Christ — came to you so that you might come to Him." We have tried to show in what sense this is a sort of central expression of the spirituality of St. Anthony. The significance of this key-word emerges also in the Saint's understanding of the sacraments. Here we will concentrate on just one of the sacraments, the sacrament of penance. We do this because frequently the theology of the sacraments is not emphasized strongly by the faithful, or even by many priests. When we speak of confession, we say: Anyone who has sinned and who stands unjust before God must go to confession in order to be made just again.

Surprisingly, Anthony speaks of confession in the following way: "All good people weep in the afflictions of this world whereas the children of this world rejoice. God's goodness has called the just to weep over their sins, to lament their sins in confession . . ." To be called to confession is quite different from saying: We must go to confession. What does Anthony mean by this unusual expression?

When we speak of confession, we commonly talk about what is necessary from our side for the reception of the sacrament. Of course, we do not forget what God does in this sacrament: The forgiveness of sin. But that is easily seen as a sort of conclusion after the more intense reflection on the human action. Anthony puts the matter in the proper perspective when he says: "Repentance is the voice of the Holy Spirit coming out of the heart of the sinner. Even though you may hear this voice, you do not know whence it comes, and you do not know how it has penetrated into the heart or how it comes out of the heart."

How little it is that we ourselves bring to the sacramental event of confession Anthony expresses in the following way: "How great is the mercy of God that it purifies a soul on the basis of repentance."

And in his distinctive style, which can be understood even by the simple people, he continues: "Christ is called a child for many reasons. For the sake of brevity, however, I will deal with only one. If you have done something painful to a child, if you have censured it or struck it, but then you take a rose or something similar and give it to the child as a gift, the child thinks no more of the injury; it forgets its anger and hurries into your arms. It is similar when you have injured Christ by your serious sins — regardless of how great the insult may be — and then offer him your repentance or your tearful confession as a flower. He thinks no more of your insult, he forgives your guilt, and he hastens to embrace and to kiss you."

Anthony gives a surprising accent to the understanding of confession when he says: "How great is the goodness of God! How exalted is the dignity of the sinner! God, who dwells in eternity, sets up a dwelling place in the humble heart and spirit of the person who repents."

By drawing on some further thoughts of St. Anthony, we would like to develop the significance of the words: "The exalted dignity of the sinner." First, we ought to recall what Anthony said about the mystery of repentance, when he stated that repentance is the voice of the Holy Spirit. But it remains basically unclear how this voice of the Spirit can be found in a person who is a sinner. For a sinner is not simply someone who has sinned, or who has done something bad. Sin does not lie simply in an action. A person who sins or who does what is evil becomes evil in himself. So it remains a profound mystery how the desire for the good can arise from the personal center, from the heart, of a person who has become evil. This mystery cannot be clarified even by psychology.

What Anthony says about the mystery of repentance is not a mere passing thought on his part. He returns to this mystery on many occasions. "The Spirit of the Lord fills the earth, because he pours the grace of repentance into the hearts of sinners and removes from them eternal woe." To this we can add another statement of Anthony that extends our vision of the exalted dignity of the sinner: "When the Spirit of grace is given to us, he floods our hearts with repentance for our own sins and sorrow for the sins of others. Anyone who mourns over the sins of others with a pious intention simultaneously atones for his or her own sins in the best way."

These words come from the conviction that neither sin nor the sorrowful turning away from sin is simply a question of the individual person. Rather, it involves relations with others. If at the beginning of the eucharistic celebration we say "I have sinned" and if we confess this in the presence of "all my brothers and sisters," then we can use the same expression — "all my brothers and sisters" — as we turn away from sin in sorrow.

Why do we speak of "the exalted dignity of the sinner" who does penance in the sacrament? Anthony says: "If the image and likeness of God in us is deformed by sin but is again impressed on the soul and renewed in it because of heartfelt repentance, God breathes his breath into the soul as into its face." Therefore, confession is similar to the sacrament of baptism; it is for us the sacrament of rebirth and new life in the Holy Spirit. This Anthony recognizes: "Confession also is a baptism of water and the Holy Spirit; of the spirit of contrition and the water of a sorrowful confession."

If all we see in the sacrament of confession is the fact that sins are forgiven, we have not grasped the sacrament in its depths. Certainly this sacrament of reconciliation is orientated in a special way to the forgiveness of sin. But there are many ways in which sin may be forgiven, especially for those who remain in that living relationship with Christ which is characteristic of the baptized. Today the consciousness of this is stronger, especially in the context of the celebration of penance.

If we wish to understand better what makes the sacrament of penance to be a sacrament, and in what way it is distinguished from the other possible means of forgiveness, we should approach it in terms of the sign-function proper to it, for all sacraments are symbolic in nature. According to Catholic sacramental theology, every sacrament has a three-fold sign-function. When this is applied directly to the sacrament of penance, it means:

The sacrament of penance is a "signum demonstrativum," that is, a "proclamatory sign." This means that, already in its external form, it reveals what happens in the sacrament. What transpires in the sacrament of penance is the judgment of God, and this is simultaneously the grace of forgiveness.

The sacrament of penance is a "signum prognosticum," that is, a "sign pointing to the future." Here already begins the decisive and revelatory judgment of God, and together with this, the acceptance of humanity into the realm of divine salvation. And, in this sacrament the human person places him or herself willingly, humbly, and in faith under the law of this judgment which frees him or her from all guilt.

Finally, like the other sacraments, the sacrament of penance is a "signum memorativum," that is, a "commemorative sign." This means that the memorial of the salvific work of Christ which was carried out in his suffering, death, and resurrection, is celebrated in those signs typical of it. Indeed, this is the most important aspect of the sacrament of penance. Anthony of Padua has said much that can lead to a fuller understanding of this.

In his explanation of the word *pontifex*, Anthony

explains what it is in the redemptive work of Christ that is commemorated in the sacrament of penance. This word can be seen as synonymous with "high priest" or with "bridge builder." Anthony begins with this double meaning for the word. He says: "Christ is called the high priest (*pontifex*) of future goods. He is called *pontifex* because, for those who follow him, he builds a bridge or a path. There are two shores which are separated from one another; the shore of mortality and the shore of immortality. Between these flowed the stream of our sinful misery. Hence, Christ appeared as *pontifex* (as both high priest and bridge builder), and himself became the bridge from the shore of mortality to the shore of immortality."

Christ made himself into a bridge. This image must be taken seriously. Every bridge belongs to both of the shores which it joins. In this case, it is a question of the shore of our mortality and the shore of God's immortality. It is clear that, as the Son of God, Jesus stands on the shore of God's immortality. But by reason of the incarnation, through his coming into our mortality, through his death on the cross, he stands also on the shore of our mortality. Thus, he is firmly grounded on both shores; he belongs to both. For this reason, and only for this reason, is it possible for his disciples to pass over Christ as the "bridge" from the shore of mortality to the shore of immortality.

Now it is not simply that we pass from our mortality to his immortality by means discipleship. Since death entered into our world through sin, the two shores can be given different names: The shore of sin and the shore of satisfaction. Anthony speaks in this way when he is thinking directly of confession: "Penance is also a passage, for we pass over the bridge of confession from the shore of sin to the shore of satisfaction."

The phrase "the shore of satisfaction" does not refer to our human action or prayer in the sacrament of penance. For, of itself, that is not real satisfaction. True satisfaction is made to the justice of God by Jesus Christ. He himself is this "shore of satisfaction" of which Anthony speaks.

What, then, is to be said about our "shore of sin?" Does Christ stand on this "shore of sin?" Here we touch on the central mystery of our redemption, the mystery of the salvific work of God which is revealed to us but which we cannot understand with human reason. And it is better if we do not attempt to clarify this mystery with human reason. But we must allow it to be proclaimed over and over through God's word. This is affirmed emphatically in two particular texts of Holy Scripture: "He sent his son in the form of sinful flesh and condemned sin in the flesh" (Rm 8:3). "He made him to be sin who knew no sin, so that through him we might become righteous before God" (2 Cor 5:21).

We would have to reflect long on this in order to grasp the awe-inspiring mystery involved. If we hold to this statement of Sacred Scripture, we have to say: As the bridge, Christ belongs to the "shore of sin." He was "made to be sin" so that, as the bridge reaching from our sinful side, he could overcome our separation from God and become for us sinners the way to forgiveness and to eternal life.

Christ carried out his redemptive work for the glory of God and for our salvation. In the sacraments, he offers us the possibility of entering into that which he has brought about, both for the glory of the Father and for our salvation. How is this related to the particular nature of the sacrament of penance?

To this Anthony says: "The Father commissioned him (Christ) to place the Tau, the sign of the cross and the memory of his passion (*memoria passionis ejus*), on the brow and in the memory of repentant sinners so that in their repentance and in their confession they would lament all the abominations committed by themselves or by others."

The image of the Tau impressed on the brow of the repentant sinners is shaped after a passage from the prophet,

Ezechiel. There, in the description of the final judgment, a man in a linen garment is commissioned: "Go through the city of Jerusalem and put a Tau on the foreheads of everyone who sighs and groans over the abominations in the city." Those who are marked in this way will be spared the horrors of the judgment (Ez 9:4).

What Anthony intended by the sign of the Tau can certainly be interpreted to mean that the more efficacious motive for repentance is to be found in reflection on the cross. But when we hear that "the memory of his passion (*memoria passionis ejus*)" will be impressed on the sinner, we become aware that we say precisely the same thing concerning the renewal of the work of salvation in the Eucharist. This is true of confession as well. There also the "memory of his suffering" takes place. It can be said also of the sacrament of penance: "We proclaim your death, O Lord, and we praise your resurrection until you come in glory."

This takes place when the sinner allows him or herself to be taken totally into that which Christ has done for our salvation in his death. The Lord's death on the cross is fulfilled in and through the sinner. Sinners are drawn into the dying of the redeemer when, in the confession of their guilt, they take a stand against their former selves, saying "no" not only to particular deeds, but to their basic attitudes and the whole of their distorted lives. In this way they turn themselves against what they have been and "kill" their former self. Drawn into the redemptive work of Christ through the grace of the Holy Spirit, the sinner then proclaims the death of the Lord who has borne our sins and who has died because of them. In saying "no" to oneself, one is drawn into this death of the Lord.

"He came to you so that you might come to Him." If we apply this statement of St. Anthony to the sacrament of penance, the first part tells us: "He came to you." Christ has come to us, to our side, to the shore of those who have sinned. We who have sinned through our own fault meet him on our side; him, who "for us was made to be sin" (2 Cor 5:21). And when we allow ourselves to be united with him in confession, the second part of the statement comes into play: "So that you might come to Him." For then, he — as our bridge — leads us through his suffering and cross to the shore of the new and eternal life of God. So it comes about that we can "praise the resurrection" in which we participate.

The memorial of the saving work of Christ takes place in the sacrament of penance, even though in a form different from that of the celebration of the Eucharist. Here also his death is proclaimed, and his resurrection is praised until he comes in glory. The startling mystery lies in the fact that the renewal of the saving work of Christ and its efficacious presence takes place in and through human persons who have been sinners of their own free will.

As a preacher of penance, Anthony was certainly capable of speaking about sin in a penetrating way. But he also proclaimed that it is precisely confession that reveals the dignity of the sinner: "How great is the goodness of God! How exalted is the dignity of the sinner! God, who lives in eternity, comes to dwell in the humble heart and spirit of the repentant person." Here, in a way, the "Happy fault" of the Easter Vigil resounds. God's merciful omnipotence is greater than sin. And that mercy makes it possible for the sinner to follow the one who redeems us from sin.

But when the sacramental renewal and memorial of the work of salvation takes place in the church, it is always something that pertains to the entire church, and is never limited to the individual person. The fact that the redemptive work of the Redeemer is constantly re-enacted in the sacraments has a meaning for the whole church.

From this perspective, the question of the "devotional confession" can be grasped. It is questionable whether it is appropriate to speak only of the forgiveness of sin in the case of devotional confession. Unfortunately, what is made to seem most important is the frequency of devotional confession. It was even said that if a person wished to go to confession but could think of no sins that had not already been forgiven, he or she should "include" sins already confessed. Precisely that is highly questionable if — as we have said — one is concerned only with the forgiveness of sin, for these "included" sins have already been forgiven in the sacrament. Nevertheless, this inclusion of sins already forgiven can be meaningful. For by this means, a person admits that he or she belongs to those who stand on the shore of sin. Even though the sins may have been forgiven, yet it remains true that this person belongs to those who have sinned. And therefore he or she can be united with Christ who was "made to be sin" for us. For this reason, in the sacrament, such a person can enter over and over again into the dying of the Lord who draws the sinner into his resurrection.

As a master of surprisingly deep formulations, Anthony says something that expresses an essential element of the confession of devotion. "God's goodness has called the just to weep over their sins, and to admit their sins in confession." A profound statement: The call to confession! According to the Gospel, every call has as its purpose that those called might be with Jesus Christ (cf. Mk 3:13), and that they might follow him (cf. Mk 1:17). We have already heard from Anthony how this companionship with and following of the Redeemer takes place in confession. A call of the just to confession! Anyone who has been made "just" through him, and who has entered on the way of his life, cross, and resurrection, must understand — precisely as one who is just — what significance it has that the redemptive work of Christ becomes an ever effective presence; a meaning which does not remain with the individual person, but works itself out in the whole of the church.

Unfortunately, these perspectives are not sufficiently taken into account in discussions about the celebration of penance. Certainly the forgiveness of sin in the sacramental celebration is discussed. But that which Anthony so strongly emphasized is not discussed: the sacramental renewal of the redemptive work of Jesus Christ in and through the sinner.

VI.
THE MEMBERS OF OUR BODY ARE, AS IT WERE, THE GARMENTS WHICH CLOTHE THE SOUL

The human body. Is it not a touchy issue today if we want to know what a saint thought about it? Will it not be a question of direct hostility to the body? For, it is commonly thought that a saint is a person who would have had a very low estimation of the body, that he or she would have felt it was necessary to kill the body in order to liberate the soul, and that a genuine saint would have encouraged others to take a negative and critical attitude toward the body. And what would the case be with a saint who lived in the Middle Ages? Above all, what would the case be with a saint who took on such severe bodily austerities that he collapsed, as Anthony did at the little cloister of Montepaolo? What sort of message about the body would he have to offer?

In view of this range of questions, it might come as a surprise to discover that Anthony of Padua clearly wished to communicate a message of respect for the body. This can be concluded from many of his statements. For example: "The good Master invites us: Come, far from the restless crowds. Come aside for solitude, solitude of the body and of the soul."

Body and soul form a unity, each influencing the other. Functions of the soul have an effect on the body, and corporal affairs influence the soul. When we are dealing with the search for solitude and recollection, as suggested in the citation from Anthony, physical exercises directed to quiet and repose can well encourage and achieve a peace and harmony of the soul. Soul and body do not go their separate ways in human life. The power of one helps the other in an organic collaboration. This means that we ought not turn all our concern to the powers of the soul in a one-sided way and ignore the possibilities of the body. On the contrary, we ought to give to each area the importance which corresponds to the proper order that ought to exist between them.

Anthony named the "five senses of the body . . . the gates to the country" of the soul. This understanding of bodily sensation corresponds fully to our human situation. Whatever enrichment and encouragement we accept and appropriate from others is experienced by us at the "gates" of our existence in the form of signals that are received by the body. Thus it is in the case of hearing where, through processes that are bodily in nature, we can receive the intellectual content of what someone else wishes to communicate to us. Contact and communication from soul to soul, from spirit to spirit, is not the ordinary mode of communication among human beings. Communication presupposes the physical ability to receive the "signals" which are sent in a bodily way from the other.

"The members of our body are, as it were, the garments which clothe the body" says Anthony. We do not come to know ourselves in a purely spiritual way. But we can come to know ourselves through the external expressions that proceed from our body. We ought, therefore, to think of the rich palette of possibilities of our bodily language.

In this mutual relation and interaction between the body and the soul Anthony sees the image of God in the human person: "As the human spirit is the life-principle of the body, so the Holy Spirit is the life-principle of the human spirit. The first imparts life to the senses, the second imparts the life of sanctifying grace." Holy Spirit — human spirit — human body: this order makes it clear, in a way, that the human body is touched by the work of the Holy Spirit, even if this takes place by way of the human spirit which is totally united with the body. This is expressed very briefly by Anthony in the following words: "The life of the body is the soul; the life of the soul is God."

From this we can draw a first, simple conclusion: "How beautiful is that order in which the soul is subject to its Creator, and the body is subject to the soul." As the soul that is united with God, its creator, experiences the full development of its possibilities precisely because God is leading it, so the reflection of God extends itself to the body when a person allows bodily concerns and dispositions to grow along the lines which the soul follows under God's guidance. This does not imply a dualistic hatred of the bodily dimension, nor does it see the body as an undesirable appendage to the soul, but allows the bodily dimension to find its fullest development in its proper ordering to the soul.

It is particularly important to Anthony that the human person as a whole should experience the fullness of salvation, not only in terms of the soul, but in terms of both the soul and the body. Citing the text of Psalm 27 (vrs. 7) "My flesh shall be renewed, I shall thank him with all my heart," Anthony goes on to say: "The human body lived in paradise before the fall. It lost its life because of sin, but it rose again in the resurrection of Christ and will be fully restored to life at the general resurrection."

It is above all the resurrection that clarifies to what an extent the body is involved in salvation: "The members of our body are, as it were, the garments that clothe the soul. We should spread these garments on the roadway, (that is, we ought to accept suffering and death for the sake of the name of Jesus,) so that someday we will receive them back in glory and immortality in the general resurrection of the dead." As we participate in our redemption by following our Redeemer's path through suffering and death to arrive at the glory of the resurrection, it is necessary that the entire person, body and soul, follows this way with Christ.

Thus, Anthony sees the resurrection of the body as an important aspect of human fulfillment that awaits us in the glory of God: "Our heavenly fulfillment consists in two things: the glorification of the soul and the body, and the vision of the triune God." It should be noted that Anthony refers to the glorification of the body and the soul as a single process without dividing it into one process for the soul and another for the body.

And he attempts to depict that glory, which embraces the body as well as the soul, in the following way: "In that glory, such a clear light will shine from our bodies that I will be able to see myself in your face as in a mirror, and you will be able to see yourself in mine; and an unspeakable love will grow from this . . . . At the present time, it is impossible for us to love each other as we should, because we are hidden from one another by darkness and are separated from one another by the secrets of our heart." Anthony clearly sees that our efforts to find genuine love are plagued by many problems in our earthly condition. And these difficulties are connected with the fact that we do not meet each other soul-to-soul with no veil between, but because all expressions of the soul are made by means of the body. Because of this, we do not grasp each other in our depths. But if our body is someday to share in the glory of God, only then will the fullness of genuine love become possible through that transparency that will be given to us. Then we will no longer experience shame when others are aware of the secrets of our heart. In fact, it is precisely through the love made possible by our final struggle that the perfection of love becomes possible. All this indicates that we ought to treat our bodies with genuine respect. In Anthony's view, this ought to have implications for all bodily necessities. He speaks about eating food. The cultivation of the table-manners is for him a religious concern. But he had apparently experienced many things that were not only rude but unreligious as well. He speaks clearly and honestly about the lack of manners in many people when he says: "They attack their plate as though it were a fortress, and they do not put aside their weapons until everything is wiped clean. They eat greedily and give themselves up totally to the business of eating, attacking their food in haste and straining their arms as though they were taking a stubborn fortress by storm."

While Anthony says clearly that the body will share in salvation because it already shares in the journey to salvation, he was just as clear about the fact that the body was involved in the first sin and labors under the effects of that sin. "The devil brings humanity into the double corruption of soul and of body." Here the body is not described as an evil power with which we must wage an unconditional battle. Rather, we must recognize that the painful bodily situation of humanity is marked by the effects of sin. What a hindrance a hungry, thirsty, tired body can be for so many of the things that we would like to achieve. How often is it not the case that the body asserts itself: "I cannot do it."

An important conclusion follows from our bodily situation: we should not work out the large plan for our life in a way that would be appropriate only for a healthy body. We should not take the position that we can serve God only as healthy people, and that anything else is a failure. Anthony expresses this in the following words: "Earthly goods and bodily health are like a reed." This does not mean that a reed cannot provide some support. Rather, it means that it breaks easily and wounds with splinters the hand that tried to find support for itself in the reed.

Our bodily situation should lead people to honesty: "Our body is poor. For it enters this land of exile naked, blind, and miserable. And it will leave this foreign land naked, blind, and crying . . . It is subjected to need and cold, it is plagued with sickness . . . Of what, then, are you proud, o poor, unfortunate man? Of what can you boast? Whatever you cannot take with you later does not belong to you." This is not just the opinion of an overly zealous, popular missionary. Strictly speaking, it is a paraphrase of the words of Sacred Scripture: "We brought nothing into the world, and we cannot take anything out of the world. But if we have food and clothing, let us be content with these. But those who desire to be rich fall into temptation, into a snare, into many senseless and hurtful desires that plunge people into ruin and destruction. For the love of money is the root of all evils" (1 Tim 6:7-10).

Those who wish to follow Christ consistently must place themselves under the word of Christ who told us that a person must deny him or herself (cf. Mk 8:34). We must cut back on our struggle and be ready to carry the cross in the path of the Lord. Since we are made up of body and soul, we ought to recall that, as the body is involved in sin, so it should be drawn into the process of satisfaction. Whatever we can do with respect to salvation ought to be done by the entire person. Therefore Anthony says: "Repentant sinners make peace with God, the Father, whom they have offended by sin. Called from honest sorrow, they enter into the presence of the King through confession, throw themselves on their faces in sorrow, practise bodily penance, and see themselves as vile and unworthy." We do not readily speak of corporal penance today. But Anthony did so. His reason was that he took seriously the unity of body and soul in the human person. We must make our way back to God in the wholeness of our reality, and not in some non-corporal, purely spiritualized form.

It is important to maintain the proper order and harmony in the relation between body and soul, and not to over-estimate the importance of one to the detriment of the other. This means that we ought not place the care of the body above the care of the soul. Unfortunately, this is often the case. Anthony complains about those who not only ought to know better, but from whom we have the right to expect that they must maintain the proper order.

We refer to the religious. Apparently with a precise knowledge of the situations in the cloisters, Anthony says: "It is
written in the rule or the statutes of their order that each
monk or canon shall have two or three shirts, and two pairs
of shoes for summer and winter. When, at certain times
and places with nobody's fault, it happens that they do not
have these things, they complain that the statutes of the
order are no longer observed, and that terrible aberrations
are involved. Behold, with what zeal they would follow the
laws and prescriptions concerning the body. But the law of
Christ they observe hardly at all, even though without this
they cannot find salvation."

When Anthony reflects on the desire that can clearly
come from the body, he is reminded of a comparison with
false prophets. False prophets offer a message that seems to
contain some truth, but they are really opportunists who
try to avoid giving any offence. Thus, the Saint says: "The
body also has its prophets who say to it: Why this fasting?
Why this torment? You will become sick; you will become
so weak that you will be no help for yourself or for others.
But it is written concerning these prophets: Your prophets
proclaim lies and falsehoods to you."

Precisely in these issues, Anthony shows himself to be
a man of absolute honesty. He was not satisfied with half-
measures; he demands an utter honesty. Thus, he says
once again, and this time even more seriously: "The desires
of the flesh are false prophets. They point out the fragility
of the flesh and the weakness of the body in order to lead
the soul astray. They preach peace to you, and point out
the great mercy of God. But they speak of all these things
only to lead you into sin."

As Anthony sees things, it is often the religious, from
whom one ought to expect the most consistent following
of Christ, who fall under the power of these "false prophets." "Thus, many people who lived quite simply at home
before they came to the cloister soon became very fussy in
the monastery." Such people "do not find joy in prayer but

in idleness and laziness . . . I mean those who dwell in God's church in leisure and laziness, seeking entertainment, gossip, and conversation instead of the quiet of prayer."

Because of his insistence on honest consistency, Anthony can become somewhat ironic. "A full stomach can well sing the penitential psalm 'Miserere.' " In this way he describes the false relation between pious language and a totally different way of life. He also says: "They first observe the strict fast on the vigil in order to prepare a feast for the body."

In all this, he was aware that such clear and unambiguous language would not be received everywhere with enthusiasm: "The teaching of Christ had a hard sound. But it does tell us to discipline the body and to despise the world. Therefore, we do not hear it gladly."

All these statements naturally involve a certain severity in life-style. But Anthony does not preach suffering for the sake of suffering. He relates it to the mystery of salvation which is characterized by the cross of Christ. Therefore he says: "Present your body whole as a sacrifice to Jesus Christ. He gave himself totally as a sacrifice to the Father in order that the body of our sin would be totally destroyed." Again, this is a question of simplicity and honesty. For how can we speak of following Christ on the way of the cross to which we are called if we are not prepared for sacrifice?

The consistent direction which Anthony represents in these matters is, in his opinion, the only way to realize the proper harmony between soul and body: "The just person deals with the body as with a slave. How fortunate is a person when the slave is so obedient that it does whatever is commanded. Then the spiritual person can say to the slave: Do this, and the slave does it." This is not a question of systematically searching for what is hard and difficult. Rather, it means that a person should not avoid the hard and difficult when it is part of the normal course of life.

We will bring these reflections of St. Anthony on the

bodily condition of humanity to an end with one of his prayers: "We ask you, Lord Jesus, pour out the light of your grace into us. In this light, let us live in accord with reason, keeping the flesh under control, so that we may come to you, who are Life. Grant us this, you who are blessed for all eternity. Amen."